Y0-BWB-872

# AMID PERILS OFTEN

## By Stanley W. Hoffman

TO
my granddaughter
**Tiffany Alexis**
who since her arrival in Uganda
has been to me a balm from Gilead.

"Since my people are crushed, I am crushed;
I mourn, and horror grips me.
Is there no balm in Gilead?
Is there no physician there?
Why then is there no healing
for the wound of my people?"
—Jeremiah 8:21, 22

# Contents

# Preface

This was to be the fifth book in a series which I am writing about my years in East Africa as a missionary. I was planning to publish them in chronological order. But my wife, especially my daughter, advised me to put this one out first. I have bowed to their wishes.

This book has been written while in Uganda. I am most grateful to my daughter for typing out my manuscripts so that they will be ready for the publishers when I reach America. In the end it became a race against time. She spent hours at the machine for my sake as I kept feeding her my scribbled notes.

The accounts in this book are written in the present tense. I want you to see and feel as I saw and felt when it happened while I lived amid perils often.

Stanley Hoffman
Kampala, Uganda
June 9, 1987

# Introduction

In 1977 we took a three-year leave of absence from missionary service and accepted a call to pastor the congregation at Carstairs, Alberta. We wished to be near our daughter Colleen who was attending Anderson College in Indiana, and to spend more time with our sons Kirk and Mark. As well, we were waiting on the Lord for direction. Did he want us to stay in the homeland and share on missions? Or, would He lead us again to the mission field and where?

The call Marion and I received to Africa back in 1958 never left us as we ministered in Canada. When Idi Amin's reign of terror was drawing to an end in 1979 my heart began to burn within me for Uganda. Sharing this with my wife we began to pray about it. We wrote the Missionary Board and were advised to wait until the situation there became more stable. We continued to pray about our return to the mission field. That He would open the door at the right time. We loved the home we had and the congregation we were serving, but the call to return to the foreign field was too strong to be denied.

One year slipped by. We continued to wait. Another year came and went. Why was it taking this long? Were we mistaken? If we were, then why was the burden increasing? The more we communed with God the more He prepared us for Uganda. He led me to read up on this land which I had visited only once back in 1970 for a few days. Tears flowed freely as I sat in my office at church studying the country He was calling me to. It ran over into my ministry in Carstairs. My feelings could not be hid. They knew someday I would be leaving them for my beloved Africa.

Then in 1982, after three years of waiting before the Lord in prayer and fastings often, God saw that the time had come to open the door for our return to Africa. He saw that we had developed sufficiently and were ready for what lay ahead of us in Uganda. Things began to happen quickly! The Missionary Board felt it was safe to send us to Uganda and the date of departure was set for the following year. A letter came from Paulo Mwendwa, a pastor in Uganda, with a plea, "Come over and help us."

Preparing for our departure we saw more and more how He had planned so well for our lives. He had allowed us to be around for the marriage of Colleen and of Kirk, and then to witness Mark's graduation from High School. His timing is never off! Had He opened the door sooner we would have missed those family blessings.

During the many days of waiting before the Lord, he revealed two things to us. The first one was to Marion, that our ministry in Uganda would be more fruitful than it ever had been in our previous years. The second was to me; that it would be much more difficult than it had ever been in Tanzania and Kenya.

As Paul had to be re-shaped during his waiting period so we too had to go through a re-moulding process. We needed to be tempered to the right degree so as to be able to withstand what was awaiting us in Uganda. When the big guns boomed from nearby hilltops and automatic riflefire whistled past us, we soon learned why the Lord had taken all that time with us. For we found ourselves amid perils often!

# AFRICA

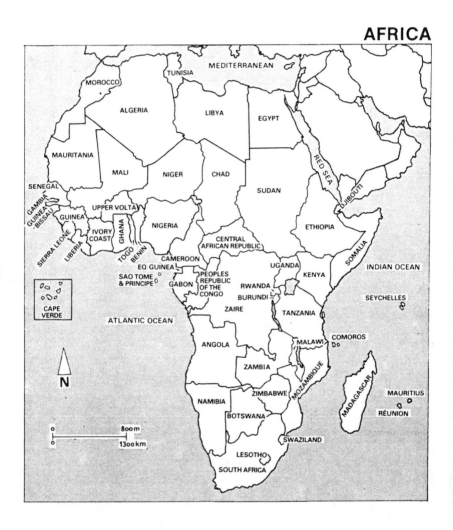

**UGANDA**

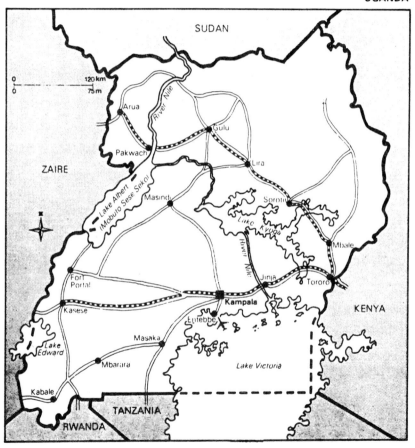

# Chapter One
# Each Step of the Way

Lake Victoria reaches up to greet us as the plane loses altitude and then hits the runway at the water's edge. Slowly we taxi into Entebbe airport. Music pours out of the cabin loud-speakers as we commence filing down the aisle. I recognize the tune. Marion and I used to sing the song years ago. It is one of Red Harper's songs—"Each Step of the Way." How appropriate! A confirmation from the Lord.

Marion and I have always been sensitive to the Lord's leading. We obeyed His call to go to Africa exactly twenty four years ago. He led us safely through the following eighteen years. Then in 1977, He led us into a pastorate at Carstairs, Alberta, where we spent the following six years. And today, July the 13th, 1983, He has led us back to Africa. But why Uganda?

When the news came in 1979 that dictator Idi Amin's army was on the run with the Tanzania troops in hot pursuit, our hearts became burdened for the black pearls of Uganda in the heart of Africa. We notified the Mission

Board that we were willing to go there as soon as the war ended. But it would take three more years before our request was accepted. The conditions in the war-torn land were not favorable, was their answer. There followed then a year of preparations before we finally bid our children and friends farewell.

Our family has always been closely knit throughout the years in Africa. This safari will be different than the previous ones. Marion and I are going without our children. In the Calgary air terminal we wave goodbye to them as we pass through the check point. And then they are out of sight. The jet lifts heavenwards. I am glued to the window. For how long I do not know. I do not want any one to see me weeping. Only God's call can sever so strong a family tie.

Frank and Margaret Lafont, missionaries to Kenya for years, had gone to Uganda in 1969 and stayed eighteen months to oversee the work. It had started five years earlier by Kenyan Christians who had moved to Uganda and settled mostly around Kigumba in Bunyoro. Soon after Lafont's departure Idi Amin began his onslaught of the evangelical churches. Many go underground to keep their identity while others seek refuge by joining one of the two powerful churches who have existed since before the turn of the century. They are by now so entrenched in politics that they escape the dictator's decree.

The Christians at Kinyonga refuse to close down their church and carry on worshipping in their little mud and wattle building. After the Liberation War in 1979, they learn of a church in Kampala which is wishing to associate with them. It was started by a pastor who had returned from exile in Kenya, where he had fled to escape the rod of Idi Amin. Soon plans are underway to ask the Missionary Board for someone to come and help them establish the church. When they learn that we are willing to come to their troubled land, correspondence begins in earnest. And here we are.

Stepping out of the plane, I thank God for leading us thus far. And I pray He will continue to lead Marion and me each step of the way. We will need it. And, by faith, I believe He will. As the song we have just heard suggests:

> I'm following Jesus one step at a time,
> I live for the moment in His love divine.
> Why think of tomorrow, just live for today,
> I'm following Jesus each step of the way.
>
> The pathway is narrow, but He leads me on,
> I walk in His shadow, my fears are all gone.
> My spirit grows stronger each moment each day.
> For Jesus is leading each step of the way.

Paul Hutchins from Kenya meets us at the airport. With him is Ephraim Tumusiime and several others. They drive Marion and me into Kampala, twenty miles from Entebbe, and book us in at Namirembe guest-house. The room here will be our home until we find a house to rent. Two days later, Paul takes a plane back to Nairobi, leaving us the vehicle which we are to use until we acquire our own. Marion and me are now on our own.

We are squeezed into a room which can just hold two single beds and one chair. Our two suitcases we must stash under the beds so that we can move around. Five days after our arrival we have a caller who is the bearer of sad tidings. He says that he has some bad news, especially for Marion. Before we can guess, he quickly adds that her dad has passed away. We are shocked! He explains that Paul Hutchins had called him to deliver the news. Having said this he leaves. With whom, besides the Lord, do we share our new-found grief? We have only each other. Dad had not looked ill when we were with him the last few days. Saying goodbye to him at the airport, he did reply to my "See you in four years," with "I don't think it will be here." I added, "It will then be in heaven." There had been tears in his eyes.

While sitting in this little room mourning the passing of a dear saint, another knock comes to our door. Opening it we find Ephraim and the pastor standing there. Inviting them inside we share our news we have just received. Ephraim wishes to pray for Marion. We lay hands on her and he offers up a fitting prayer which is filled with compassion. God brought these two messengers of peace along at the right moment! He does not forsake His own. They minister words of comfort to her who has just heard that her beloved father has departed to the realms of glory. Marion does not wish him back, for he is now home.

The abrupt change from western Canada to Uganda is shocking to say the least. The roads and streets are appalling! Pot-holes are everywhere. Some huge enough to bury in them our little car from Kenya. Travelling back and forth to town is not only rough on us but the vehicle as well. There is no street that has escaped destruction. The smashed tarmac with ragged edges sends us flying as we maneuver the vehicle through them. It is unbelievable how the roads have deteriorated! We see no one repairing the damages. Though the Liberation War ended four years ago there is still instability in the country. No one is concerned about road repair as yet.

Many buildings and shops are empty. Others are severely damaged. Those that are operating do not contain the items which the sign outside says. Instead of a photo studio, it is used to sell packets of groundnuts, sugar and salt. The streets are lined with squatters peddling their wares, from tattered weatherworn books to strips of rubber tubing and metal strappings. They take up most of the sidewalk forcing you to step around them.

God only knows why the Kampala residents are not dying of cholera. There are heaps of garbage piled up along most streets. Goats and cattle feed on top of them. The stench is unbearable as you drive by. Buildings are stained and in need of paint. Charcoal smoke has blackened the tops of many windows all the way up the wall. The panes are smashed or missing.

Soldiers with automatic weapons loiter in the streets. Others pass by in loaded Landrovers and lorries. One must constantly be on the alert as no one knows when a convoy of them, escorting either the president or some other official, will come screaming up in front of you or behind you.

Coming down the street from the Standard Bank to the Post Office, I hear sirens! Where is it coming from? I see Elijah motioning me to move off the street. I glance behind me and see a cavalcade approaching led by two motorcycles. Their lights are flashing and sirens blaring. Cars are parked along the street I am on so I can not pull over. Cannot go to my right due to the cement divider. The sirens are ringing in my ears. One motorcycle squeezes by me, waving me to get out of the way! But where? Then an open Landrover containing armed troops lumbers by, the wheels on its far side on top of the divider.

I glimpse an opening between two vehicles and shove

the Datsun into it and up on top of the sidewalk. The Landrover halts at the end of the street broad-side to the Post Office and men spill from it with levelled guns covering us all. Everyone on the street freezes. Is this for real? Or am I watching a play? That automatic weapon he is pointing in my direction, only fifty feet away is the real thing! The black Mercedes pulls by me. Cannot see the president inside as the windows are covered. As soon as it is past, plus the rear guard of soldiers, the ones on the street holding their drawn machine guns then jump into their vehicle and speed after them. What an exhibition!

On another occasion as I pull into the round-a-bout at the Clock Tower, sirens commence blaring, notifying the civilians to give way. The stream of traffic on the inside lane halts immediately. I am on the outside lane which happens to be where the on-coming convoy is using as well. I see the headlights of the leading army vehicle flashing in my rear view mirror as it roars up behind me. He brakes in time to avoid running into me. Finally I am able to scoot out of their path and they rush by me. Fortunately for me the lead vehicle does not stop to reprimand me as one did at another round-a-bout in a similar situation. The soldier had jumped out and jabbed the rifle butt into the face of the man in a white V.W. who had not gotten out of the way quickly enough.

I find myself sitting in someone's office daily. Days drag into weeks. Ephraim and Elijah assist me in the search for the countless places I need to find. Hours are spent waiting in dark hallways where the bulbs are missing and the smell of backed-up toilets fill the corridors. Staring up at the ceiling I wonder whether the tiles hanging by one corner will drop while I am there. The offices are bare except for a table and a chair or two. The answer we receive is familiar. "Come back this afternoon," or "He will be in tomorrow." I return to Namirembe after the offices close, which can be anywhere from two o'clock to four o'clock in the afternoon, leg weary from climbing up and down flights of stairs because the lifts do not work.

It takes me a few weeks to discover that the skin irritations I have are caused by fleas. They are here in the guest-house! In spite of using insect spray which nearly kills me, they keep attacking me. Marion is not bothered by them! I am covered with welts from their bites. And do they itch! For six weeks I endure them and then finally I am forced to vacate Namirembe. I cannot stand the itching any longer.

Where do we go to now? As yet all the house hunting we have done, and have looked at many, has been fruitless. To add to our dilemma, I come down with malaria. We ask God for direction to a place where I will be free of fleas. Packing our two suitcases, plus a few handbags, into the vehicle we drive down the road. Where to now Lord?

Before long the thought comes to Marion that we should visit a couple of Canadian doctors who are living in an apartment on Makerere University campus. She was given the names and addresses before leaving for Uganda. We were to look them up.

We locate the two couples in Lincoln Hall and are invited into their suite. During the course of our visit, we learn there is an empty apartment just above theirs that needs sitting while the tenants are on short leave. They prefer missionaries to occupy their suite. Here was the answer to our prayers! He led us right to the place! Praise His wonderful Name!

# Chapter Two
# Guardian Angels

The Bible says that we saints all have one or more angels whose job is to guard us in our pilgrimage while in this world. For in Psalm 34:7 we read, "The angel of the Lord encamps around those who fear Him, and He delivers them." Again in Psalm 91:11, "For He will command His angels concerning you to guard you in all your ways." I have read these portions of scripture now and then without taking too much notice of them. That was until our guardian angels began making themselves known to us here in Uganda. I do not recall them being so obvious while serving in Tanzania or Kenya. But with life so dangerous in Kampala, they could not help but be seen on our compound. It gave us the assurance we needed that the Lord was with us, that we were not alone out here in this land of turmoil and unrest.

When we arrived in Kampala, we immediately booked in at Namirembe guesthouse on Mengo Hill. Then began our search for a house to rent. Four weeks went by and during this time we would hear gunshots at night and people screaming as they were being robbed or molested. One night soldiers entered the guesthouse compound and ordered the kitchen staff to bring them food which they took with them. We quickly learned what Kampala is like—an unsafe city!

Eventually we locate a house we like. It is on Muyenga (Tank Hill). It overlooks Kampala. It does not take us long to move our two suitcases from Lincoln Hall on Makere Campus where we have been staying the past four weeks. How will our first night be in this big empty house? Are there thieves around here as well? Will we hear gunshots tonight? We commit our lives into His care as we retire for the night.

Several nights later both Marion and I are awakened at the same time. It is two o'clock in the morning. What we hear is not loud but different. A scratching sound. Not nearby, but from the other end of the house. I slip out of bed and tip-toe my way along the hallway in the dark. Approaching my office I hear this peculiar noise coming from within. The door is locked and the key is back in the bedroom. Listening at the closed door I still cannot decide what it is. Is the night watchman sharpening his panga (knife) on the cement walk outside? Or, is there a thief inside the room?

Without wasting anymore time I step to the side of the door and rap sharply on it, shouting "Wewe ni nani?" ("Who are you?")

If it is the watchman, he will reply. If it is a thief, well, who knows what he will do. There is no shot. Only silence greets me. I rap on the door again, louder than the first time. Still no response. It is then that I have the feeling that it was not the watchman but an intruder!

Going quickly to the front door I call the watchman by name. No answer. I return to the bedroom and call him

20

from the window. Still no reply. To my second outburst the day worker awakens and answers me. I take the torch and key and head back to the office. Marion tells me to be careful. The intruder may still be around.

Shining my torch into the office I find no one inside. But I see the screen on the window slashed on the bottom and top. After the light has been switched on we see how the thief had almost gained entry. I interrupted him just in time. He already had unlatched the bottom of the screen and was now ready to undo the top. The pane in the metal window had been removed so that he could turn the handle to open it. Several of the flat security gratings had been snapped off by twisting it with his bicycle wrench, I would guess. He was all set in a few moments to pull through the radio which is standing on my desk. Thank God for awakening us when he did.

Where was the watchman? He is now standing outside the broken window along with the day worker who had to awaken him. No, he had not heard the thief nor me calling. Yes, he had been asleep.

The nights are noisy in Kampala. It is not from vehicles which disappear off the streets after dark. Rather it is gunfire we hear sporadically throughout the night. Some distant and others near enough to awaken us out of our sleep. Often it startles Marion so that she pops upright in bed awakening me in the process. The clanging of tin cans and women screaming tells us that another home is being broken into by thieves. Marion and I peek through our window and listen. Which house is it this time? I wonder how many are doing the same thing? Peering out from behind locked doors, not daring to go out there empty-handed to face a gang which shoots to kill. No one calls for the police. They never seem to have a vehicle when needed.

Dogs add to the nightly ruckus of Kampala. They commence as soon as it is dark and carry on until well after midnight. They bark, howl, whine, growl, yelp and yap continuously for hours on end. Are they rehearsing a choir number? I am sure I have heard them harmonize on several occasions. This idiotic frenzy breaks off sharply at the crack of a gunshot nearby, only to resume when there is a lull.

Besides gunfire and barking dogs, there is also the music blaring forth from local pubs. Every weekend it is enough to keep you awake all night. A good cover for the thieves who do strike more often when the disco music is booming into the night skies from giant speakers.

Whenever we hear gunshots nearby, a question comes to our minds, "Will we be attacked as well?" I assure Marion that God will protect us. But she wants God to give her that assurance. She prays and asks God for a sign of His protection over us and our possessions.

That very night the watchman sees, just after midnight, animals enter our compound. (When he described them to me later they fit those of horses which he had never seen before). They each carry a rider. Several stay at the gate while the rest proceed on up towards the house. As they draw near to where he is sitting he rises up to stop them. They vanish! He sits back down and the horsemen re-appear. Only this time they are two deep! He arises and is about to call me when they disappear again before his eyes.

When daylight comes he asks for an interpretation of what he had seen. I tell him he has had a vision. God had revealed to him that guardian angels were encamped about us. There were more than enough to protect us. He should not be afraid but know he is not alone out there at night. They are watching with him. Marion has her sign, the confirmation she sought!

There were times I would go on safari up country for seminars without Marion. She was either busy with something at home or did not feel up to another trip so soon after one we had just completed. It was not the best thing to do, leave her alone, but there was not any other choice. The work was young and I needed to be out in the field. What helped was that she believes in God's protection and stands firmly on what Psalms 91 says. This made it possible for us to be separated days on end.

While away in south-western Uganda for a week, Marion has two callers one night during my absence. She is awakened at four-thirty by the watchman tapping on the guestroom window. He does not come to her window as it faces the gate. There are two men with guns outside the gate he tells her. Marion looks out her window and sees them. Then the outside security light reveals them crawling over the gate and drop inside the compound. And they are carrying guns!

She grabs the whistle lying beside her bed and proceeds quickly to the kitchen which faces the house above us. There they have a security guard on duty at nights. She commences to blow her whistle as loudly as she is able hoping that the guard above will hear and come to her assistance. But there is no response.

Returning to the bedroom she looks out and sees them crouched over, moving up towards the house. Then the thought comes to her to switch on all the lights in the house. As she moves from room to room she is praying for His assistance and protection.

Our watchman, in the meantime, is peeking around the corner of the garage and watching the two gunmen. When they get mid-way to the house from the gate they stop suddenly. Then turning abruptly they run back to the gate, climb over it, and disappear into the night. What had happened? Why had they turned and fled?

Returning from my safari a few days later, Marion tells me what had taken place. It is a miracle that we escaped being robbed and her getting molested. Thank you Lord, for watching over her and our home! Who but You could have assisted her.

That night I find myself standing in front of the house at the bottom of the steps. I see four figures in white poised between me and the gate. They are facing it as if watching for something. I stare at them so as to discover who they might be when they commence to fade away. It is then I spy two other figures. These are in black, coming up and over the gate and into the yard. They proceed up towards the house in a crouched position.

When about mid-way to the house the white figures re-appear to stand in front of the two in black. I can just distinguish them as the four in white appear now to be transparent! The two in black halt. Then they turn and flee. Those in white remain and are totally visible again. It now dawns on me that these are angels! I begin praising the Lord and shouting, "Hallelujah! Hallelujah!"

I want to run to them and thank them. But I cannot move! I increase my efforts while at the same time still shouting out my praises and thanksgiving to them. Then I hear Marion calling me. She wants to know what the matter is as I was thrashing about and groaning out loud.

It is a vision I have had! The Lord has revealed to me what had happened the night the two gunmen had come to rob. They had turned and fled the compound because of the guardian angels standing watch. They must have seen them! And I too had the privilege to look upon four of our guardian angels on duty here at Muyenga. Hallelujah!

# Chapter Three
# Foiled Attempts

Before we learned to keep the smaller gate within the larger one locked as well, unknown callers walked in unannounced. We suddenly see him, or them, standing at our open door. The watchman learned eventually not only to keep the gates locked but also to refuse strangers entrance without our permission. This precaution had to be observed as questionable characters did call on us, before and after security measures were put into practice.

Looking up from where I am sitting in the living room I see a man standing at the front door. He is a stranger. Now why did the watchman allow him to come this far without announcing his entry? Nothing to do now but invite him in. His story is that his wife and son were killed by armed men in military uniform early this morning around two o'clock. He was not home but away on duty as a watchman for some Mzungu (white man). He has no one to turn to for help so he came here. He needs money to buy burial cloth for his wife and child so as to transport them to the morgue. The police will not allow the dead to be in a public vehicle without the bodies wrapped in burial cloth.

Now why did he come across town to share this urgent need with us? According to the description of where his place is situated, it is on the other side of town! To come here he passed the big cathedrals of the Church of Uganda and the Roman Catholic. Also, the Full Gospel Church is right near his home. I ask him why he came this far, how did he know about us? He tells us that he was told by the Church of Uganda that we will help him, that we are good people and help those in need. "What about your boss, the Mzungu, can he not help you?" I ask him. "He's away, had to go to Canada quickly," he replies.

Is he telling the truth? Or is it a trick to get money out of us? "How much will the cloth cost?" He gives me the figure. "Did you report this to the police?" I ask. He says that he did and was told to bring the bodies over to the morgue. "But," he goes on, "I need the cloths before I can do that." Is this for real? Marion suggests I drive over to check whether it is so. "We're doing wrong by refusing this man help if his story is true. And if it isn't, then we have exposed him." Is it alright if I come to look at your late wife and child?", I enquire. That is fine with him. He will direct us there right now.

I take with me one of the watchmen, and stop on the way to pick up the pastor of our group of believers. In spite of living in the same locality as the stranger, the pastor has never seen him before. To this the man explains that he is a recent arrival and that is why. A short distance from the pastor's place he asks us to stop the vehicle. We are not far from the Full Gospel Church. We now walk he says to his place. "It is not far off the road."

After walking for ten minutes we turn sharply to the right and then two minutes later we come upon a road. He has been acting as if he is lost. Keeps looking to the left and then to the right. "What's wrong?", I ask him. "You lost?" "No," he says, "It's just that I'm still new here." The road we are standing upon I recognize. Why did we not come this far with the vehicle? Is he leading me away so his companions can steal it? "I'm going back to bring up the vehicle," I inform the rest. It is not far. The road leads me to the vehicle which is still where we left it. Thank the Lord! Did I return too soon?

Picking them up I carry on down the road for some distance before he directs me to turn off onto a smaller one. This road ends at some huts. "Is this the place?" "No," he says, "It's in that direction." His original story as to where he lives is gradually falling apart. In fact, changing as time goes by. He either is really a stranger in the area and thoroughly mixed up in his directions, or not doing an excellent job of leading us far enough away from the Datsun that his companions are to steal.

We ask the locals in the village whether they had heard any shots last night. Yes, they had. "What time?" "At ten o'clock" is the reply. "Any around two o'clock in the morning?" "None." "Anyone die nearby?" "Not that we've heard." We do not hear any wailing. Did anyone really die? We have come this far, let us see where he takes us next. The villagers are asked to keep an eye on the vehicle while we are gone.

He leads us along a canal that flows out of the papyrus swamp ahead of us. There are a few huts to our right and I expect him to turn off to one of them. But he does not, instead he keeps staring ahead and heading for the swamp. Beyond it I recognize one of the hills as part of residential Kampala. We have made a half-circle and are now looking south! "Where is your house?" I ask him when the last hut is passed. "It's just beyond this swamp," he answers. "What! You mean we have walked all this way and your house is on the other side? Why didn't we drive on that side right away? Why come around this way only to end up having to cross through a swamp? It doesn't make sense!" He has no answer.

I talk it over with my two companions. They think he is leading us into a trap. He has accomplices in the swamp who are waiting to club us and rob us of everything including our clothes. As for me, I still have the feeling he is using delaying tactics to give his associates ample time to remove my vehicle. I foiled it earlier by returning unexpectedly. They need time to re-group. Our stranger here is doing his level best to accommodate.

While we have been discussing the issue, he has been waiting just out of earshot. "We are going back," I tell him. Strangely enough he turns immediately and is ready to head back to the village with us! No begging us to press on! He surely should have tried to persuade us to complete the journey if his house is really out here. Especially if it contains his late wife and son whom we came to see for confirmation of his request for help. It must be true that he is one of a gang of thieves!

Hiking back to the village along the canal, I make sure he stays ahead of me. I shoot a glance behind me at the swamp repeatedly. Nothing moving. The stranger does not say a word all the way. No protesting. No pleading. Only silence. Odd! At the village I walk directly to the vehicle, thankful to find it intact. An older lady calls the pastor aside and tells him in her language that we should have nothing to do with the man. "He's no good," she says, "He wishes only to steal your Mzungu's motor car!"

Meanwhile in the vehicle I have a few more questions for him as I have made up my mind to drop him off at the police station. "At which police station did you report the incident?" When he tells me which one, that is where I will take him. But he says, "I didn't go to any." "You told me that you reported it to the police." "Yes. I met him on the road. It wasn't at a station." With that reply he slips the rest of the way out of his original story! And out of the car as well.

Do I pursue him? He is not taking the same road we came. If I should be able to overcome him and manage to drag him to the police, what do I tell them? I see him turn off the road and slip into the heavy brush. He is gone.

As we pull into the yard, Marion and the rest of the workers are waiting for us on the front veranda. She is relieved to have me back unharmed. "Soon after you left," she says, "I got a heavy burden to pray for your safety." She immediately had called in the workers and asked God to protect us from the unknown dangers that had beset us. They had prayed until the burden was lifted. God answered their prayer. He foiled an attempt to trap me in order to steal the vehicle.

Returning from Kapiri in Teso we take the by-pass at Jinja. It has countless potholes but we are in a hurry to reach home before dark. Midway on the bypass we spot a soldier ahead of us. He is frantically waving for us to stop. Rufus and Ephraim are along and the latter advises me not to give him a lift. The soldier does not look friendly and Ephraim is suspicious of him. Driving by him he shouts at me to halt. Glancing in my rear view mirror I notice he has his gun raised and is sprinting after us.

I stop the vehicle. He approaches and demands we take

him along to the next roadblock which is at the dam. I oblige since he is holding a gun. But when we arrive at the place he said that he would disembark he remains in the car. Seeing the soldier inside the men at the road-block, who also are men in uniform, wave us on without a delay. While crossing the dam which spans the Nile River at its source, our passenger attempts to conceal his weapon behind him on top of the back seat. I am beginning to be suspicious of him myself! Is he a rebel? Or a deserter? Who is he?

At the check point on the west side of the dam, which is manned by the police, we are stopped again. Marion and I are asked to identify ourselves. We show the officer our passports. Next Rufus and Ephraim are asked for their identity papers. Then, to my surprise, I am asked whether the soldier with us is in our employment. "No," I answer, "We just picked him up on the by-pass." There is an instant change in the officer's attitude, "Where is the permit to that gun you have here?" he enquires of our passenger. The weapon had not escaped detection.

The soldier fails to produce the required document. In a flash the door is flung open and he is yanked out of the Datsun. His arms are pinned behind his back while another policeman removes the rifle from inside and commences to flip out the shells from it. All this is done so swiftly that the rest of us are momentarily stunned. We are relieved when the officer orders us to carry on with our safari. Ephraim offers a prayer of thanks as we speed away.

The soldier had not been willing to leave the vehicle at both roadblocks. Why? Was he actually out to steal the car as Ephraim suspected? True, we are now entering a forest where he could easily have dumped our bodies after killing us. During the reign of terror under Idi Amin, many of the victims were hauled here in lorries and left to decay in the shadows of the mivuli trees. We narrowly escaped sharing a similar grave.

We praise the Lord for undertaking and delivering us in a miraculous way from this dangerous situation. Another attempt to steal our vehicle has just been foiled. The Psalmist wrote: "Surely He will save you from the fowler's snare." (Psalm 91:3) Amen. How true!

# Chapter Four
# Commandeered Into The Bush

We have been in Uganda only a few months and already we have met many roadblocks, especially on the roads we travel to reach Kigumba. They are manned by soldiers of the UNLA, the ragtag army of president Milton Obote. These men are always in dirty fatigues and lack manners. Old tires, broken wheelbarrows, branches and pieces of metal are used as barriers. All pack automatic weapons with extra clips of ammunition taped to their guns, many of which have no stocks.

Roadblocks are spaced apart from a couple of miles to as many as twenty or thirty. We have to carry our passports with us each time we travel. The nationals must have their identity cards on them at all times. They also need to carry extra money with them besides the amount for the fare as at the roadblocks they will be asked for "chai" (tea) or "sabuni" (soap) by the soldiers. We have seen passengers lined up behind the bus identifying themselves one by one to the man with the gun. Should the passenger have a chicken or a stock of bananas on top of the bus, immediately his chai is increased.

Our policy is to hand the soldiers tracts only, even when they have asked for chai. We then answer that the written Word is more satisfying, it contains the Water of Life. Tracts are readily accepted, and will even ask for them when they know who you are. Life at their roadblocks must surely be lonely and monotonous. Knowing Swahili has helped us many times as most in the army understand and speak it. This tells them we are not newcomers whom they can easily bluff and intimidate.

One must constantly be alert while traveling the roads as often the barrier is just a stick or two lying in the middle. The soldiers manning it may not be in sight either. They are loafing in the shade somewhere. We never travel after sunset. Too dangerous. One could never spot the barrier in time as there are no flares. Vehicles have been fired upon and people killed when they happen to drive through unawares.

Leaving Kampala on Bombo Road I see the barrier ahead of me at the next curve. I drive slowly by as there is no one present. Must not be an important one. Less than a mile further a car shoots by us with an arm sticking out of it's window flagging us to stop. Two men with their guns hop out and hasten to where we are parked. I hear one say to the onlookers, "Thought they would get away!" One squeezes in beside my wife while the second one sits in the back seat along with our passengers. I am ordered to return to the roadblock.

Nothing is said on the way. Only when I see the officer in charge do I explain why I had not stopped. Checking our passports and the passengers' identity cards he is satisfied that we are harmless and allows us to carry on with our safari.

We have been warned that there are certain road-

34

blocks which are not legal but are set up by renegades or guerrillas. How to tell them apart? Driving in Kigezi district on one safari I see ahead a rather suspicious barrier. There ought not to be one out here! Two surly chaps wearing a different shade of fatigues are engaged in a conversation with some locals near it. I decide to go on through. As soon as I do I hear one bark out an order to halt! Looking into my rearview mirror I see him with a raised gun. I halt and reverse back.

He is furious and asks whether I had seen the barrier. I let him furnish his verbal barrage. He adds, "all the black people out!" Then he asks for chai. I offer him tracts. "How can we eat these?", he complains. I hop out, open the rear door and pull out several bananas. The ruffian has followed me expecting to be handed some money when out of sight of the others. He is shocked when I offer him bananas instead. Grunting something he turns away in dusgust. His comrade meanwhile is laughing at the whole affair and comes over to take the bananas. We continue on our safari without another incident.

Motorists often had their watches removed besides their wallets. While driving on the main street of Kampala I am flagged down a block from the post office. Not by a soldier but by a policeman. He is not interested in the vehicle registration or my driver's license, as much as what I am wearing on my hand. He points at it and says "Give me that, I want it." I point to my watch, thinking that is what he means. But he reaches in and touches my ring. I reply, "No, that is my wedding ring from my wife" and drive off.

We are on our way back to Kampala from Kinyonga. We just spent a weekend with the Christians in that area. While there we met a lady who had come from a place where some others want to meet me. Would we stop in on our way home? We had been asked once before to pop in but were unable due to a lack of time. I agree to this safari since she is along to guide us to the village. We left early from Kinyonga for this purpose.

A couple of miles after crossing the Kafu River we came to a dirt road which branches off north into the bush. The lady asks me to turn onto it. As soon as I do, three soldiers appear further up the main tarmac road. They are running, shouting and waving at us to stop. I obey. Approaching us with levelled guns, we are ordered out of the vehicle. After inspecting the inside, for guns I suppose as they don't ask us for our identification, I am commanded to drive the car up to their camp a short distance away. Marion, our two house girls, and the lady follow on foot escorted by the remaining two soldiers.

Their camp consists of a vacated hut and a lean-to. There are at least thirty soldiers present, most of them already drunk from the "pombi" (local brew) they are drinking. Here I undergo further questioning by a tall soldier, wearing sunglasses, who apparently is their officer. He wants to know where we are going. I explain that we have been invited to meet some Christians further on in the bush about five miles. When he asks for the name of the village I have to ask Grace, our lady friend. Learning that she comes from there, he commences to interrogate her. It is obvious now that where we want to go is off limits to travelers!

The officer in charge decides that I take three of them and Grace to the village we intended to visit. It's to check whether our story is true. One of his uniformed friends cautions, "Waache" ("Let them be"). He is ignored. All our communication is in Swahili. I am ordered back into my vehicle and Marion, who had re-entered, to get out.

They need the space. She and the two girls are to remain in camp and await our return. I immediately object to this. I am not about to leave my wife behind in the company of drunken soldiers.

The officer repeats that there is no room for her. The car is a Datsun and it's true there is not enough room for everyone. I say to him, "She is my wife and she goes where I go. I am taking her with me!" This is the show down. If they mean us ill it has to be here and now. Not out there in the bush where no one will ever find us. I have nothing to lose by sticking to my rights.

The officer stares back through his sunglasses. Then relents. He turns to the third soldier and makes him stay, muttering that two of them is enough. But the two girls, Annah and Mary, are to remain in camp. I again speak up and tell him, "Haiwezekana!" ("This is impossible!") He wants to know why. I reply they are our hired help and I am responsible for their welfare. They can wait out at the main road but not here in camp! He ponders a minute and then consents. The girls then walk out to the tarmac where two locals are waiting for a bus.

Grace is shoved into the back seat and a soldier sits on either side of her with their weapons. The officer has lighted up by now and I stop him as he is about to climb inside. I tell him no one smokes in my vehicle including him. He can't believe it! Pauses a moment, then drops the cigarette reluctantly. Now why did I do that? Wasn't it tense enough? Any wrong move, or word, can set off the spark that will ignite the whole thing!

When we hit the dirt road the two start to grill Grace with all kinds of questions. She answers them calmly. She keeps repeating that there are only Christians back there in the village wishing to see the missionary. Then why have they not been notified of this meeting? She answers that as far as she knows the church leader has notified the local officials. Why they at the road haven't been notified, she doesn't know.

Their interrogation becomes heated and the two begin to slap her on the face. I spin around and shout, "Hapana!" ("No!") He answers me sharply, "Are you challenging us in performing our duty?" I reply, "Why are you so high-strung? We have no weapons as you have. We are people of peace." To that he retorts, "So are we for peace. That's why we are out here." I respond with, "Peace can only come from within. Weapons will not bring lasting peace." I go on to add that we are Christians and that Grace is saying the truth. Besides, she is a lady and should be treated as one. To that they say that Museveni the guerrilla leader is using women in his intelligence, especially those of his own tribe as Grace was. Thus the rough treatment. I tell the two they are jumping to conclusions.

A mile down the road we enter a village. Here the officer wishes to enquire whether they know the woman. We stop in front of a shop where a group is loitering. The soldiers remove Grace from the car and march her over to them. They are asked by the officer whether they know the woman. Silence. Then Grace addresses them in her own language, "You know me!" The second soldier, not understanding what she has said, hauls his hand back to strike her and shouting at the same time, "Don't you know Swahili anymore?" But seeing me pop out of the front seat he manages to arrest his swing before his fist lands on her face. What would I have done had it landed?

When the group is asked again whether they recognize her, one replies, "No, we don't know who she is." With that the two bring Grace back inside the vehicle. "See, she is not known here. She is a liar." I know better. They did know her, but were intimidated into denying her. The cowards! I am now ordered to keep going on into the bush where she wants us to go.

We travel less than a mile and run out of a road. Then we follow a track which leads us northwards. Finally we are on just a footpath. The surroundings we find ourselves in now reminds me of hunting days in the Tanganyika bush. There should be wild game around, especially elephant and buffalo. I ask the soldiers whether there were any, to which they reply, "Ndio" ("Yes").

I fail to see any. Probably all shot out by them. It's sad not to see wildlife in these many miles of empty bushland. They at one time were here but have since been wiped out! The same applies throughout the rest of Uganda, excluding the parks. And even they have been so emptied.

The officer who has now clamed down asks me where I picked up all my Swahili. In Tanzania, I tell him. He then informs me that he has spent six years there. We now have something in common! Having maneuvered a mile along the crooked pathway, I begin hearing a knocking on the front left side of the car. I mention to them I have to stop and investigate what is making the noise. The second soldier gets out with me and when I get down on all four to look under the front end he does the same, laying his rifle within a few inches from my hand!

I discover that the knocking comes from the arm which is attached to the body and the tie-rod apparatus. If this were to go out of commission we would be stuck out here in the middle of nowhere for days! I inform them that we must turn back as the rough terrain will increase the problem. The two talk it over and then agree for us to return but the woman carries on with them. I am not happy with their suggestion. Put the car into gear and keep moving. Grace says it's only a couple more miles.

It's slow and steady over the bumps now. Try and favour the left side as much us possible by keeping that tire on the path. I can tell Marion is praying that we will make it. Fortunately, she has remained quiet. Since the soldiers have commandeered as into the bush she hasn't said a word. That's not like her really. She is not afraid to converse with them, and has done so on occasions whenever we have stopped to give them a lift. Once when we were full, she said to the soldier who kept persisting, "Can't you see there is no room?" No, she is not afraid to talk to them. But I'm glad today she's praying instead of talking.

Ahead of us is a bog. The Datsun will never tread that. What to do? While contemplating our dilemma, three locals approach on the path from the other side. One is pushing a bicycle. We notice it's knee deep as they slush across to our side. Grace exclaims she knows the man with the bike! With that the second soldier jumps out, confronts the man and snaps, "Do you recognize this woman?" Will he be intimidated as well?

Glancing over at us he replies that he does. God bless him! He is then asked whether he is a born-again Christian, to which the reply is, "Yes." That seems to make a big diffference to the man in uniform. We have found as well that here in Uganda it is not enough to just ask whether he or she is a Christian. You also add the phrase "born again" or "saved." The word *Christian* has simply become to mean religious in this country.

The believer is then asked if it is true that there is a

Christian meeting planned in his village. He replies there is. Then why haven't they, the military, been informed? "The church leader has notified all the officials," says the man, "we did not know that the army is supposed to know as well." The officer then orders the man with the bike to return to his village and fetch the church leader immediately to their camp.

We now turn around and retrace our way back, praying that the vehicle will reach the tarmac safely. Even the two in the back are now silent. The knocking continues. Finally we arrive at the main road. The girls are still standing where we had left them. It is now two in the afternoon. At this rate it will be dark before we reach Kampala. One cannot speed with a wheel that is ready to wander off in it's own direction at any time.

The army men tell us we are free to leave. Grace is kept there. They are going to wait for the church leader now we are told. The woman will be released as soon as her story is verified by him. He is to explain as well why he didn't inform them of the planned meeting in a restricted area. I'm guessing that they will not let him off until he has paid them for the mistake.

Picking up Annah and Mary we point the Datsun in the direction of Kampala. Our speed reads fourty kilometers. A mile later it reads fifty. Where is that knocking? I do not hear it! Neither does Marion. I gradually push the speed up to my normal driving. Still no knocking. Praise the Lord! The knocking was brought about in the bush by Him! To help us get out of there. Otherwise we may have had a major catastrophe happen to us. God only knows. But this we do know that he has other things in store for us. He saved us from a dilemma while being commandeered into the bush.

# Chapter Five
# Shall Trouble or Hardship
# Separate Us?

Thieving is almost a way of life here in Uganda, especially in the capitol city of Kampala. To own luxuries is unheard of by the majority of residents where necessities alone are difficult to acquire. The cost of items are too high for the wage earners. To survive many turn to looting their neighbours or employers. He who owns a radio dares not turn up the volume lest a passerby is tempted to steal it. To be poor is the norm. For as soon as you purchase something, you become a candidate for night callers. I have listened to Christians here in Kampala testifying of how God saved their lives from thieves who broke in and stole everything they had, leaving them only the breath they were breathing.

We have not escaped entirely their notice either. One morning, I crawl into our Datsun (the Nissan has not yet arrived) and commence to pull out of the driveway in front of our flat at Makerere. I immediately notice a wobble in my steering. Do I have a flat? To my amazement, I discover all the wheels are without nuts! Each tire is facing in a different direction. Had I gone another foot, the wheels would have dropped off completely.

Why the thief took only the nuts, I do not know. Was he spooked away before he could remove the wheels? I thank the Lord for saving me the tires and rims. Catch a mini-bus which takes me down town. The shops do not handle what I need, so I walk to the market called "Shauri Yako" (your affair) but also named the Thieves Market. Here I find the nuts I am searching for that will fit the Datsun. Mine which were stolen should be appearing here tomorrow. It is still too early.

At the city market, where we do our shopping for fruit and vegetables, are young lads who wish to carry our basket. Most of them are orphans, and have learned the art of stealing to perfection. I return home one day and notice the cap for the petrol tank on the vehicle missing. Which one of the little rascals was it? Actually I have found one or two who are sincere and worthy of the extra we give them for assisting us in our shopping. I will always remember the one who wept when he discovered I was being cheated by a peddler from whom I was purchasing some goods. I was touched by the real tears he was shedding. I had become his friend.

Leaving the vehicle locked, I entered a shop a few doors down in search of spare parts. A few minutes later I am back at the car and discover the door has been jimmied. The key refuses to enter as well. A pedestrian standing in front of the shop informs me that someone had been attempting to enter my vehicle. His key had almost fit, but not quite enough to unlock it completely. When he saw me come out of the shop he made a fast exit. Had I not returned when I did he may have been able to pry the door open as he had told the pedestrian watching him that he was working for me.

Before I drop off my two pairs of trousers at the dry cleaners, I wander over to the post office for the mail. Returning to pick up my trousers I find them gone! I check all the windows and find they are closed properly. The doors are locked as well. Now how did they manage to disappear? Whoever he is, must have a key to the Datsun. May the trousers serve him as well as they have me. I brought them with me from Canada.

While I go down into the Thieves Market, Marion stays behind in the vehicle. Mary and Annah are with her. We now have our new Nissan and are not anxious to part with it. While I am shopping for several items, I hear gun fire coming from the street above me. I rush up the stairs in time to observe several men in plain clothes placing someone in the back of a white pick-up and speed away.

I find Marion safe, but all shaken up from what she just has witnessed. Several men had approached a civilian at a shop and commenced questioning him. Then they began beating him with iron bars. When a crowd gathered one of the men with a rifle fired a shot, wounding someone in the shoulder. This thinned down the on-lookers. When the man they were beating kept struggling, he was shot. Thinking him dead they heave him onto the pick-up. But the man shows life. He is promptly yanked off, as you would a dead animal, and shot again point blank while lying on the ground. He is thrown once more onto the vehicle and hauled away. The man did not move again.

*     *     *

Leaving Marion with the vehicle, Rufus, Gideon and I set out on foot to hold a service at one of our new points. It is situated on a stretch of grass-land in the midst of a marshy swamp. To get there we must first cross a river. Several months ago I baptized twenty six candidates further down stream from here where the water is crystal clear. It is sandy and I could see bottom. A good thing! It assisted Rufus and me in keeping an eye open for lurking crocodiles. They have dragged a dozen head of cattle to their doom recently. We completed the service without a mishap.

We strike off in the direction of the village a mile ahead. It is mid-day and the sun is hot. Marching briskly we make good time, passing several huts along the way. Then we are at the river. Here it courses through the marshy section and is muddy. There is tall grass and reeds along both banks except for a clear patch where man and beast cross. Our path that will take us to the place of worship picks up again on the other side.

There is a dug-out canoe resting on our side. Gideon mentions he knows how to operate it and will ferry us across. Rufus and I remove our shoes, roll up our trousers and step into the muddy water. Gideon, who is bare foot and wearing shorts, gets to the dug-out ahead of us. The cattle coming to drink and pass through, have dug up the bank with their hooves. We sink to our knees in the slush while pushing along the vessel before it agrees to float.

It wobbles as we pull ourselves onto it. Sure is shaky! Gideon grabs the long pole and shoves the dug-out into deeper water. We begin to reel from side to side. "Are you sure you know how to run this outfit?" I ask him. "Oh yes," he answers. We jerkily approach mid stream.

There are no paddles for this thing, so we cannot assist Gideon. He is propelling us along with the pole by sticking it into the river bottom and pushing on it. The further we move from shore the more he has to lean over for leverage. He is either too tall for the pole, or the pole is too short for him, for suddenly he is off balance! The pole is stuck in the mud and he is unable to straighten quickly enough to keep up the rhythm. Over we go!

I manage to keep my head above the water. Then my feet touch bottom. I am standing in shoulder-deep water. Glancing around I discover Rufus grabbing the boat. Gideon is alright as well. I was able to hang onto my Bible when I went over but it is soaked. No use crawling back into the canoe which has been righted by Gideon. It will just roll over as soon as we try it. I strike out for the other side, holding my wet Bible and shoes, which I have removed, above my head. I am as wet as I will ever get anyway.

The water reaches my chin when I am mid stream. I keep walking. It does not get any deeper, and finally I am wading up the opposite bank, my toes digging into the mud to keep from slipping and sliding. The other two are not far behind. I empty my pockets and lay out the shilling notes along with the Bible to dry in the sun. Rufus spreads out his contents as well which includes his identity card.

Nearby Christians, seeing our plight, have sent over basins of clean water which we use to rinse the mud off ourselves and our clothes. Very thoughtful of them. By the time we arrive at our meeting place, which is under a big tree, my clothes are nearly dry.

What about our return trip? Gideon volunteers again, says he now has some experience. But Rufus and I say, "No, we will walk." But we do not have to for the owner of the dug-out is present when we arrive and he takes us across without a mishap. We find Marion waiting for us at the vehicle. I am thankful she stayed behind. Upon hearing what happened she too is thankful to have escaped the dunking in a muddy river.

*　　　*　　　*

It is the rainy season. But that is no reason to stay off the roads. Even in Bugisu. Here Mount Elgon rises 15,000 feet in eastern Uganda bordering Kenya. Beautiful water-falls cascade down the rocky crevices, some of them dropping thousands of feet. A marvelous sight! We have entered some of her caves on the Kenya side, great enough to room a herd of elephants. And they do go there to seek the salt-like substances found inside.

The Bagisu skirt Mount Elgon on the west and south sides, while the Sebei nestle on her northern plateau. We have churches in both tribes. The roads are treacherous to navigate during the rains. Without the four-wheel drive of our Nissan Patrol it would be impossible to reach many of our churches in the remote corners of Uganda. Roads in these areas have deteriorated due to lack of maintenance. Tackling them is grueling, testing the hardiest vehicle, and driver, I might add.

I am on my way to visit new churches on the slopes of Mount Elgon in southern Bugisu. Besides Rufus, I have Francis Makosia with me. Marion is sitting this one out. Francis is our evangelist for eastern region. He is strong and able to traverse the mountain sides evangelizing his tribesmen. Never tired, but always anxious to look over the next hill. Where Elisha acquired a double portion of Elijah's spirit, Francis has acquired a double portion of Rufus' energy. God has used him to open the door for us into many of the tribes in the east. And he is willing for God to keep leading him into still others. I enjoy being around him. He has vision! I thank God for this man.

Francis is now guiding me to these new churches. We are on a road I have not traveled before. It is gradually getting muddier the further we climb the slope. It has rained quite a bit just recently by the signs of it. I did see the dark clouds covering the mountain, but had hoped it would miss wherever we were going. But it does not. Must have been a cloud burst, plus more added to it! I have the Nissan in four-wheel and keep plowing ahead.

Approaching a bridge in the bend we discover it severed on one end. The water cascading down the notch in the mountain side has washed it away. A foot path leads off to our left and crosses it down stream below us. I steer the vehicle off the road over the bank's edge and hugging the descending path, reach the torrent. Francis and Rufus wade through and it is knee deep. They inform me it has a stony bottom. I have no trouble maneuvering the vehicle through the churning water and over the slippery rocks.

Less than a mile later I notice, in time, and avoid dropping into a cut-away on the left side of the road. Water gushing across has washed away part of the road! Had it dropped in with the left tire the vehicle would have been pulled over the bank and down we would have tumbled to the bottom. Fortunately I was traveling slowing due to the mud. Because of it we are also losing much daylight time. There is just enough space on the right to squeeze between the hole at the road's edge and embankment.

Finally Francis says we are nearing the place where we will be spending the night. A good thing, as it is getting dark. But there is a steep hill we must climb before we arrive at our destination. I have been plowing axle-deep mud for the last mile or so. Will the Nissan be able to ascend to the top on tires all clogged with the sticky stuff? I give it a try and make it two-thirds of the way up. Then I am spinning. Back up and give it another try. Get to the same spot and spin out. Their pushing does not help.

It is now dark. To keep trying when there is no light is fool-hardy. I may slide off the road altogether while reversing! It was close the last time. Then there is the danger of getting totally hung up. With this I decide to pull the vehicle to a level spot and park it for the night. The place we were to go to for the night is just over a mile away. I send Rufus with Francis to inform them of what happened. The two are to stay there the night and I will sleep in the Nissan. "What about food tonight?" asks Francis. I tell him I will not starve. I have a few bananas and groundnuts with me in the vehicle, plus water.

Francis is reluctant to leave me alone in the dark on the slopes of Mount Elgon. But I assure him I will survive. It is not my first time to be in a predicament like this, and it probably will not be my last one either. With that he and Rufus walk on up and over the hill carrying their bags and shoes. I unroll my sleeping bag and before crawling into it, eat a couple of bananas and a handful of groundnuts. It really is dark tonight here on the side of the mountain! Just you and me, Lord.

At midnight there is a knocking on the window above my head. Opening my eyes I see a light outside. Peering out I spy Francis with a lantern. After I have the door open he tells me he just could not leave me here without some food. So he brought a kettle of porridge mixed with milk. It is about all he could really carry in the dark over the slippery road. Two Christians from the church have escorted him. I thank him for the food and tell him I am fine. I believe he was more concerned as to my safety than my appetite. Had to have an excuse too see how I was faring. Bless his heart.

Before sunrise I begin to hear passers by. They are on their way somewhere. May as well get up myself. Slept fairly well. I am believing the Lord will safely take me back out to the main road. There are heavy clouds rolling down the peak which means more rain as soon as it warms up at mid-day. Waiting for Rufus and Francis to arrive, then I will be moving out. Need to get by that cut away in the bank before it widens, and over the stream before it deepens. The visit to these churches up here will have to be re-scheduled. If I fail to get out of here in the next couple of hours, I will be stuck in this corner of Uganda for more unprepared nights.

Shall trouble or hardship separate us? With Paul I answer "No, in all these things we are more than conquerors through Him who loved us. For I am convinced that neither death nor life . . . nor powers . . . will be able to separate us from the love of God that is in Christ Jesus our Lord." (Romans 8:37-39).

# Chapter Six
# Blood Poisoning

As a rule I don't pick up chiggers. But recently I have had several. They got under my toe nails and on the sole of my right foot below the big toe. Marion had to dig in for them twice. After the first batch, others bore in deeper. The constant itching revealed they were there. She discovered them and removed them. Must have picked them up while bathing in the outdoor enclosures which they erect for us when we come for seminars. A week ago we returned from a seven-day safari which took us through Bukedi, Teso, Lango and Bunyoro districts. Could have picked them up at any one of these places.

Chiggers, while not causing serious disease or death, can be very annoying. The female burrows into the skin of the toes, generally near the nail, and lays eggs there. Intense itching occurs, and may be followed by infection and much loss of tissue and even of the whole toe. Sometimes the soles or hands are infected. They can be removed by enlarging the entrance hole with a needle, or better still a safety pin and then lifting the chigger and eggs out on the pin. In the presence of many chiggers, kerosine applied to the feet is an effective way of killing them.

Friday, and time to leave for south-west Uganda. The Lord willing we will be gone eleven days. When the vehicle is packed with those things we'll need for the seminars in Kigezi and Ankole, we have prayer with the workers and commence our safari. Rufus is accompaning us. An hour later the warning light for the fuel filter comes on and I pull in at Masaka to have it cleaned. Our first service is at Nyakitabire and we arrive there in the evening. I preach on the "Ark of Safety." Many are interested. We are on an escarpment of about six thousand feet. It is cool tonight. They get frost here now and then we are told.

We hold another service this morning. About eighty gather beside the houses. Before I preach on Joshua 24, Marion and I sing a duet. Earlier she had told the children a story. Thirty come forward for salvation. They flock around us as we pass out tracts, many pulling them out of our hands. There is an eagerness here for the written Word. Since our arrival to Uganda, we have seen over and over again a real hunger for literature. Young people run along side the vehicle as we drive away.

After a bite to eat in Kabale we strike out for Rukungiri passing through some beautiful valleys with cultivated fields all the way up to the top of the alpine hills. Many papyrus swamps have been dug up and planted. We reach our church at Kasaroza, a few miles out of Rukungiri, at mid afternoon. Soon many have gathered and after some singing Rufus delivers the message. We visit until late.

Marion tells the children a story in the Sunday morning service where nearly one hundred are present. My message is on "Following in His Steps." Many students are present from Rukungiri and they have many questions for me after the service. They are searching. In the afternoon we go to a small river nearby and twelve follow the Lord in baptism. Over three hundred spectators have gathered to witness an act they have seldom seen. After we return to where we are staying I lead a man and his wife to the Lord.

While visiting in the evening, sharp pain shoots up from the bottom of my foot where Marion had previously dug out the chiggers. The needle-like pain reaches up to the top of my arch. This is repeated a few times before retiring. In the morning my foot throbs and there is a rednesss on the top of my arch.

There are fourteen students enrolled in T.E.E. here and I am busy with them all forenoon. Take time to run into Rukungiri for some fuel. It's expensive! The highest I have paid anywhere in Uganda! Pick up some foodstuffs before returning to Kasaroza. The shops aren't much to look at just boarded up shacks. On the way back I buy some "kuni" (firewood) which is being sold beside the road.

I drive out to Kitunguru in the afternoon while Marion stays to teach the women. This new church lies fifteen kilometers away over and around several hills. We meet on one hilltop where over one hundred gather for the service. Most want prayer after the message "The Ark of Safety." Then there are questions and more questions to answer before we are able to leave. Manage to get back before dark.

The following day, Tuesday, we drive further west over more hills, some of them quite steep and arrive twenty kilometers later at Murehe perched on the top of a pass. My foot is inflamed and sore. Had to remove the shoe as it was pinching the swelling on my arch. Here we hold a service and three accept Christ. There is no free time as questions are many and when the time comes to retire it is a relief to get off my feet. Marion and I are sleeping in the Nissan which is clinging precariously to the side of the steep hill on Godfrey's parents' yard.

Wednesday finds us going to another new church which is twenty-two kilometers away at Nyakashenyi. Here I drive up the sharp hill to get to the meeting place. The vehicle leans dangerously as we circle to get to the top. About fifty turn up to hear the message on the "Light of the World" and three accept Christ. It's a forsaken area, quite isolated tucked away near a forest. After the service we walk to a house where we are given a meal, and learn that many worship idols in their homes or shrines built on their property. After we return to Murehe we carry on down to the river where Rufus baptizes seven men and women. I sit this one out as my foot is hot and swollen from being on it so much. Before retiring I had the leaders lay on hands and pray for it.

On the morrow my leg is better with the swelling down. It definitely is an infection as the result from unclean water at the Sunday's baptism getting into the opening where the chiggers had been. We still have one more service further west to attend before we can turn our way homeward. This is at Kibimibiri, thirty-three kilometers from Murehe, situated near the Ruwenzori Park. We have left the hilly country and are now in the western arm of the Rift Valley, which embraces the lakes—Tanganyika, Kivu, Edward, George and Albert. The mighty Ruwenzori mountain range is off to the north-west hidden in the haze.

In spite of my removing the shoe to keep from irritating the infection, the drive has done it no good. It looks bad! The pain is excruciating. Over sixty have showed up for the service which is under a tree on someone's compound. We go into it immediately after all the greetings have been completed. While waiting for my time to preach I keep the foot out of the shoe. But slip into it without tying it when I get up to deliver the message. Will I make it through? My foot is on fire!

It isn't long and I'm lost in the sermon "Walking with God." I feel no pain. When the call for repentance is given fifteen come forward. A church committee is then chosen and we pray over them with the laying on of hands. After the prayer is completed and I'm sitting again, it is then that I think of my foot. Yes, the pain is returning. But thank God it was gone during the deliverance of His Word!

Before we are allowed to leave, we must stay for the food they have prepared for us. There is a little bit of everything. Women peek around the corner of the door to see if the "Wazungu" (Europeans) eat the food set before them. By the time we return to Kasaroza in the evening my foot is very swollen and hot. Soak it in cold water awhile. Can't get the shoe on anymore. Someone lends me his thongs. Is there a boil forming? Before going to sleep Marion bathes it in hot water with some disinfectant she has along. This should help draw it to a head if it is a boil.

We are scheduled to be at Rutoma in Ankole for a seminar this weekend starting today. My leg is somewhat better. The forty kilometer trip gets rougher and tougher as we enter into a seldom traveled area. It is tucked away behind a ridge of hills near a river. To get to the site of the seminar we pass through plantain groves. There is just enough space to squeeze through with the vehicle. At some corners I have to reverse and maneuver around in order to keep going ahead. We finally reach our destination. But it's not with the Nissan. For the last couple hundred yards our equipment for the night is transported in on foot.

I tried to use my other leg as much as possible while driving but still it was too much for my infected foot. I ask for a place to lie down so that I can raise up my swollen leg. The room is small and contains only a home-made wooden bed. Marion and I are to spend the nights here during the seminar. They won't hear of us spending it in the vehicle. Spreading out the sleeping bag on top of the bed I stretch out for a quick nap.

I am awakened by a blowing on my ear. Turning to see what it is I glimpse a rat! It scurries up the wall near my head. He had been preparing himself to lunch on my ear. In spite of living my childhood years in a rat-infested house back in Saskatchewan, I never did get used to them. I detest them almost as much as I do snakes. Decide then and there to sleep in the vehicle. I'm not in shape to stay awake all night keeping a rat from nibbling off my ears. Back in Tanzania I was told rats will blow on the sleeping person's flesh to numb it before commencing to chew away at his ear or toe.

There is a service on the yard before nightfall. After some lively singing by school children, Marion shares and then Rufus preaches. Nearly one hundred are present. Before we retire there is more singing inside the house and finally food to eat. It is a relief to settle down in the vehicle for the night. Am finding it uncomfortable sitting with my aching leg. Yes, I was able to persuade the owner of the house that we needed to be near the various items we had left in the Nissan during the night. Never did tell him about the rat.

The swelling didn't go down during the night and I wake up with a foot that is beginning to discolor. All forenoon I teach classes. Ephraim is the interpreter. This is his home area. Marion walks to visit his parents a few miles away. Then late afternoon we all file out to the river for the baptismal service. There is papyrus every-where and the only water I see is muddy. I ask Rufus to do the baptizing again. Can't walk in there with my infected foot.

Hundreds have come to watch the baptism. They have not seen it done by immersion and laugh hysterically each time a candidate rises to the surface. It greatly affects the newly born-again Christians. So much so that only six go through with the ordinance. The crowd cannot be controlled. I have never witnessed anything like this before. The expression on their faces is fiendish with many mocking. Darkness abounds in this place! May the few candles that have been lit dispel some of it.

Ephraim preaches to the crowd that gathers at dark. Then they come to us in twos and threes until we go off to bed. Pray for eleven of them, four for salvation. As we ate our supper many sat watching to see if we really eat what they eat. The stomach and intestines were a real test, I admit! Matoke made from plantains is the staple food here. Groundnut sauce goes with it to give them some proteins. My foot is none the worse tonight in spite of the hike out to the river and back.

The Sunday morning service is held outside the little church building they have erected as over five hundred show up to hear what the mzungu has to say. They have never seen one come out here to this valley! I preach on, "As it was in the days of Noah" and eighteen come forward for prayer and salvation. The crowd line up along the bush road and wave to us as we depart. Children stream after the vehicle until they finally tire. What does royalty have over on us?

We are loaded down with several kinds of bananas, millet, and a live chicken, besides our T.E.E. books, Bibles and luggage. At Kinoni we stop for the night. This is where we hope to eventually start a church as well. It isn't until eleven o'clock that we turn in for the night. We are given a room in the owner's house. Rufus and Ephraim are given lodging as well. My foot is very swollen and discolored.

After breakfast we leave for Kampala and arrive at two o'clock. There is some mail for us at the post office which includes two tapes from the kids. Listening to them tonight is like having them in our living room. We miss them so. Colleen reads a Mother's Day poem for her mom which is touching. We find all on our compound fared well during our absence. We thank the Lord for keeping watch over the place and for His safety on the roads as we travelled. There were several roadblocks along the way but they gave us no trouble.

My leg resembles a stove pipe. I can hardly believe it is my own foot! It has swollen twice the size. The sore on top of my arch is dark and I notice a black line is creeping upwards along my calf. There are a couple of lumpy spots as well. Can it be blood poisoning? Marion prepares a charcoal poultice and ties it on my foot. I also pull a sock over it to keep it in place for the night. We hear gunfire outside. Didn't have any of that on our eleven-day, one thousand two hundred kilometer safari.

The poultice did wonders during the night. When Marion removes it this morning there is so much drainage! The painful pressure is gone and so is most of the swelling. There is still a hard swelling on my calf so Marion renews the poultice. While in town I check with a doctor and he confirms what I suspected—septicemia, or blood poisoning.

With God's help I was able to complete my scheduled safari to southwest Uganda. And with Marion's help I was saved from a worse case of blood poisoning which could have proved fatal.

# Chapter Seven
# Persecuted, But Not Abandoned

We met Arthur immediately after arriving in Kampala. He was schooling and when he ran out of funds we gave him a part-time job on our compound. His cousin Godfrey joined him and worked as a watchman until they both went on for further training at Kima in Kenya. They are boys from Kigezi which is in southwest Uganda bordering Rwanda and Zaire. They invited us to bring the gospel to their district which needed it. Though most of the Bakiga are religious, they said, their countrymen lacked the born-again experience. The message we preached they needed.

It did not take long and we had nine churches growing in northwest Kigezi. But the formal churches in the area were not pleased with intruders. Since the expulsion of missionaries and the closure of evangelical churches by Idi Amin, the two large formal churches who were allowed to continue monopolized the country and became very possessive of territories. More and more they vied for political power among themselves as well. With the overthrow of the dictator, and the gradual return of the missionaries, the formal churches now felt threatened. But we who believe in a spiritual conversion, saw only the fields ripe for harvest. Most were religious, yes, but dead in sin.

It was wonderful to see many now leave their formal churches and accept worshipping in homes or just under a tree on some hill. They enjoyed their new found faith enough to make the decision willingly. Most of the converts are young people looking for something more than what they are seeing in the established churches around for a century. In spite of the reprimands from the church elders, and their parents as some disapprove, they continue to follow Christ. Many enroll in the T.E.E. studies.

Museveni the guerrilla leader hails from Ankole just north of here. He has many recruits and sympathizers throughout south and west Uganda. Therefore the government looks suspiciously upon any gathering that is not of the norm. Thus, it is not long before the Christians are called guerrillas, Museveni's men. Those who resent our presence there make the most of this propaganda. The district commissioner is friendly and ignores the rumors. But it is damaging. Church leaders find it difficult to invite new comers to their services held in homes or under a tree. "Where is the church building?", they are asked. They do not attend, afraid they will be suspected of being guerrillas.

The persecution of the church gains momento. Church leaders are asking for letters from me to verify they are preachers of a legally registered church by the central government in Uganda. Local chiefs nudged on by opposing church elders are seeking to restrict the pastors in their movements. Evangelism is being hampered. We gather with the church leaders in seminars and visit as many of their congregations as possible to encourage and strengthen them. They hang in but it is tough.

The opposing faction becomes bolder. At one seminar while we are sleeping in our district chairman's house, stones land on the tin roof! Marion and I are startled awake, but not away. At the very next seminar at Kasaroza, while seated at the table with all the T.E.E. students, our evening meal is interrupted by stones hitting the tin roof. It bangs and rattles! Several of us rush out immediately but in the dark the culprit escapes. They have resorted to stone-throwing. Our chairman reports it to the district commissioner and he tells us that he will look into it.

Then the chairman is accused of collaborating with the guerrillas. Men come to his home to search for weapons which reportedly he is hiding. Finding none they commence beating those present with their rifle butts. The Christians scatter but not all escape the lashing and flailing. Arthur's mother is slapped and told," You old woman, what are you following this religion for?" The father of two T.E.E. students is knocked down and whipped, badly bruising his arm. When it is all over, three men are led away in custody. They are the pastor, the injured father, and the district chairman.

It is three miles to Rukungiri where they are being escorted under guard. On the road spectators are jeering at them, even shouting, "Kill them! They are guerrillas." Regarding their accusers the three discover many familiar faces belonging to those who have been trying to close down the church from the beginning. "Is this what their religion teaches, to hate your neighbor?" says Ignatius the pastor to himself, "I'm glad I'm not one of them anymore. Lord, be with us."

During this time I am unaware of their plight. I have just had blackwater fever. My first time ever. I am convalescing at home.

The three are locked up in prison after thoroughly being caned. Their backs are raw and they are unable to sit. At night they must be on their stomachs in order to get some sleep. The pastor keeps trusting in the Lord for deliverance. Throughout the following two days the guard hears them singing and praying inside the lock-up. Finally after three days they are released from custody. Two to return home and one, the chairman, to be transferred to a military prison at Mbarara. The officials are too suspicious of him yet.

While there he is interrogated by the army and tortured. One day he slips out a message to a relative to inform her of his imprisonment. She sends the word to me of his plight. But the telegram is so worded that I fail to comprehend that he is even in confinement. As I am still recuperating from blackwater fever and too weak to travel, I send Elijah who is now the pastor here in Kampala, to check into this urgent call for help.

He returns to brief me on what had taken place in Kigezi. The church has been closed and the Christians imprisoned he was told. I immediately send for Ephraim who is the executive secretary and we plan a trip to Kigezi. I am not fit to be on a rough road and my mouth is full of fever blisters not yet healed, but I must go to see for myself. At Mbarara we discover the prisoner has been released on bail and staying at his relative's place when we stop there to enquire.

The man has changed. His former outlook is gone. And so is his salvation! He blames the church for not coming to his rescue. Being rather shallow previous to this experience, his lack of faith does not sustain him when he is removed from his two companions. Keeps on insisting that the churches are closed and no need of Ephraim and I to go to Kigezi.

But we do go. The Lord strengthens me for this long jolting journey. We arrive at sunset with many questions soon to be answsered. Are the churches really closed? If so, where are the Christians? In hiding? Has Ignatius turned his back on Christ as well after his release from prison? What about the elderly man? How is he reacting? Is the chairman associating with the guerrillas as he is being suspected? Will the authorities now say that the rumors are true concerning our young church? What will they do to us? And what about Arthur's mother? She has always been so hospitable. Will she invite us back into her home? Well, here we are. We will soon see.

The little old lady comes out and greets me warmly. Overjoyed at seeing me. Yes, she had been beaten and even hauled before a magistrate where she had to answer many questions. Why did she join the new church? Why did she welcome it onto her premises? Why did an old woman like her leave her former religion? What is wrong with her? If she wished to return they would accept her. But she told them all, including her former church officials that she was following Christ. He alone can save. She told them they need to repent and accept Christ as their Saviour as well. With that they let her go. Told her she had gone crazy.

It is not long and the pastor arrives. I see a change in Ignatius. He has grown spiritually! He praises the Lord for delivering him from his confinement. His countenance is one of joy and gladness. There is no resentment as with the chairman. The whole ordeal has made a spiritual giant out of Ignatius! Where he was quiet and shy, he now possesses boldness. Yes, he is still leading the flock here at Kasaroza. And he has gone to some of the other congregations to check on them. No churches have closed down, they are all intact! Praise God!

What about the father who had been beaten? He is at home nursing his wounds and has not made an appearance in church since their release from jail. He is now scared and is staying home. His family comes and his one boy is still interested in carrying on with his studies to be a pastor. But his second son has fled, to join the guerrillas. He is afraid to return as they are still looking for him. He had hit back at the men when they had his father down and were beating him.

Sunday came and the people gathered in the building used for services. The Holy Spirit immediately is present to lift us to a higher plain. Here is an example of a New Testament church! In the face of persecution it has stood the test, and become stronger because of it. Instead of closing the door, the opposition has only driven the believers closer to their Master, Jesus Christ. And He has protected those that were His, and those that were not fell by the way.

Sitting in the service, I am deeply moved. The singing is heavenly and their testimonies touching. And Ignatius so wonderfully leads the service. Tears well up in my eyes as Arthur's mother and two other older women dance around their pastor praising and thanking the Lord for delivering him from prison and bringing him back to lead them. Sitting there and soaking in the blessings I am thankful I have come. I would not have missed a service like this for anything. To see the radiance of the Christians who have just come through being persecuted for His sake!

"We are hard pressed on every side, but not crushed; perplexed, but not in despair; persecuted, but not abandoned; struck down, but not destroyed." (2 Corinthians 4:8, 9)

# Chapter Eight
# Blackwater Fever

Rufus and I are in the West Nile. It is January and the weather is hot and dry. The rocky hills reflect the rays of the scorching sun above us. Food is scarce. The people of Alur are just ekeing out a living. We pass several sandy streams but they are dry. We meet girls with pots on their heads carrying water gotten from the holes dug into the bed of the dry stream. The only food we see at the small roadside markets is mangoes, and even they are puny in size.

We arrived here yesterday from Lango where we had a weekend seminar at Apongokisa east of Lira. The very first night there, just as Rufus began to preach, the wall on the one side of the church collapsed inwards right on top of the people. It happened to be the side where the women and children sat. The gust of wind created by the falling wall blew out the lantern on the platform. In the complete darkness children began screaming and mothers shouting for help to find their babies.

Fortunately I had my torch but it did not do much

good due to the mass of bodies moving about. Gradually order was restored, with the exception of one soul still digging among the rubble for her still missing child. The boy eventually showed up. He had stepped outside moments before the wall fell. We thanked God that no one had been killed. Only four received injuries with no broken bones from the falling mud blocks.

It took some time to quiet the crowd. They said the devil had done it. Especially when it was learned that some handbags containing clothing had been stolen during the turmoil. After much prayer they finally conquered their fear. The wall had simply given way to the pressing crowd outside who wished to look through the open windows. The shoving and pushing which took place was too much for the newly erected structure.

Got only a few hours of sleep that night as there was loud praying and singing by the church leaders until after midnight. They resumed again at six the next morning. As well, I was awakened during the hours in between, when I heard people moving round the hut where Rufus and I were sleeping. They were burning the grass and the red glow of the fire lighted up the inside of my room. Asking them in the morning what it was all about they informed me that red ants had invaded the place. Had they not deterred them by starting the fire I would have been overrun by the fierce ants! Fortunately for me as well that they did not burn down the hut in the process as the roof was made of grass.

In spite of all this the seminar ended well. The Holy Spirit blessed in the classes and in the services. Saturday and Sunday nights I showed films on the life of Christ with six hundred attending the first night and one thousand the second night. Twenty-five were baptized Sunday afternoon in a spring a short distance away. A new congregation was started some miles from Apongokisa. God was with us!

To get here to Alur in the West Nile, we had to drive most of the day (Monday). The road is full of huge holes and washouts! It led through the northern portion of Kabalega National Park, previously known as Muchison Falls National Park, where we saw quite a few animals. There are hartebeest, waterbuck, bushbuck, reedbuck, kob, buffalo, warthog and baboon. Even saw a tsetse fly which got inside the vehicle. Got rid of it in short order.

The trip was hot and dusty. Even the wind, what there was of it, gave no relief. There is much burning of grass in Acholi country and dust-devils graced the skyline. Arriving at Pakwach on the Nile River I was ready for a cold drink to quench my thirst. The water I have taken along from home is no longer cool in the thermos. We tried all the "dukas" (shops) but they did not have any cold soda. We carried on to Pamora arriving an hour later at our destination. Before we retire for the night we hold a service in front of a hut. Nearby stands a shrine recently erected to worship their ancestral spirits. My message is "Jesus is the Way, the Truth, and the Life."

This morning after tea and bananas we head out to our first place of worship. At a small market I nearly drive over a man who is bound hand and foot, hobbling on the road in front of me. I am told he goes mad when drunk so they tie him up! He charges the vehicle. I have to make a detour to get around him. Many onlookers but they are all passive about the whole incident.

At Ndrosi we open a new church. Quite a few have come. We meet on a big slab of rock under a wild fig tree. I preach on "Where Are You?" Seventeen accept Christ as their personal Saviour. Two are enrolled in the T.E.E. program.

Then we carry on to Pangere where we open another church under a tree. It is on the side of a hill just three miles from the Zaire border. I preach on "The Kingdom of God." Here twenty-one come forward for salvation. One enters the T.E.E. studies. Before we leave we are invited into the home of the newly appointed leader of this congregation. They give us a glass of local coffee spiked with lemon.

Our third service is at Acer which is on the other side of a range of hills. Here we meet under a tree on top of a knoll. A good sized group is present. I preach on "Walking with God" and seven ask to be saved. Two enter the T.E.E. studies. We rest a few minutes in an old man's hut. He is a remnant from the colonial days and feels it an honor to have me inside. He gives me a short history of the area around here. A European passed through here years ago, he says. I drink the cup of milk and eat the handful of groundnuts offered me before taking leave of the old man.

On the way to the fourth meeting place we stop at a dam to check whether it contains enough water for baptism. There is some but very muddy. The baptismal service will have to be postponed until the next safari. At Pagot which is tucked up in the hills I preach on "Listen to Jesus." The result is twenty-one come up for salvation, and two enroll in the T.E.E. program.

The Holy Spirit has been guiding us throughout the day, opening new churches and providing leaders who wish to study the Word. Arrive back at Pamora at eight surprisingly fresh in spite of no solid meals all day and preaching four messages.

We finally eat our first good meal around ten o'clock. No, I do not go to bed now. Not yet. About four hundred have come to view the films I have brought along on the life of Christ. I show two of them. It is midnight before I rest my head on a pillow. In spite of the lateness of the hour it is still hot. And because of mosquitoes I am using a net which makes it even more suffocating.

A new day. More heat. It has been like this since leaving Kampala six days ago. Load up this morning; the generator, boxes containing films, Bibles and T.E.E. books, plus my traveling bag. I am on my way back home. Before we reach Pakwach a stop is made at Alwii where we open yet another new church. Here thirteen accept Christ after my message. One enrolls in the T.E.E. studies. We do not linger around after the service as I need to get back to Kampala by nightfall. Home is still a long ways away!

At Pakwach I fill the vehicle with diesel. It is much more expensive out here than back in Kampala. It is twelve noon and stifling hot! While passing through the park we again see a lot of game. Crossing the Ayoga River which flows into the Nile, I cannot resist the temptation to stop and refresh myself a little by washing my hands and face in the water. Ended up by drinking some of it as I was parched. Hear hippo further down stream but fail to see them. Rufus does not join me but remains with the vehicle.

Finally we reach the tarmac, the road that leads to Kampala from Gulu. It is a welcome sight. The passage from Pakwach to Karuma Falls has been hard on us. The lack of food all day yesterday has left me in a weakened state. I found the road bumpier than usual. At Jeja, near Kigumba, I turn off the tarmac and drive four miles in to drop off Rufus a Kinyonga where he is staying when not on the road. Stay only long enough to get a drink of water and pick up two passengers wishing a ride to the city. In twenty minutes I am travelling again.

Before reaching Kampala we pass through eight road-blocks. Some of them are a nuisance. At one the soldier wants to know what I have inside the boxes. Even asks what is in a bag of maize the passenger brought with her. As if he does not know. I tell him so. Looking at the chicken I was given for Marion, he enquires, "Hii ni nini?" ("What is this?") I arrive home at seven, just at dark. Marion fared well during my absence.

Seven days later I wake up with the beginnings of malaria. Take a dose of chloroquine for it. Feel sluggish and feverish. In spite of it I am in the office all day. Work has piled up. Tonight we listen again to the tapes on the Bible. Got to the end of chapter twenty in Numbers. Very interesting.

I have a poor night. Tossed and turned due to the fever, with chills towards morning. Temperature over one hundred and two degrees Farenheit all day. Drink plenty of liquids and in the evening the fever comes down some for awhile. But shoots up again tonight. It appears I have got malignant malaria and blackwater fever. Marion is applying cold foments to my forehead to keep me from burning up. Listen to the end of Numbers on tape tonight.

I had blackwater fever, along with malignant malaria, three and a half months ago which left me in a very weakened state. In all my previous years in Africa, I had never contacted this ailment before. Blackwater fever, state the specialists in tropical diseases, appears only in areas where malignant malaria is common and usually affects Europeans who have repeated attacks. Males have proved to be more susceptible than females. Attacks are often brought on by a large dose of quinine, as well as overexertion and exposure to chilling. It has an average mortality rate of twenty-five to fifty percent.

The disease gets it's name from the fact that the urine assumes a black or dark colour due to the presence of hemoglobin, the colouring matter of blood. It starts with a sudden rise in temperature to one hundred and three degrees or even higher. Backache occurs, together with other aches and pains. There is an urgent desire to void and the urine becomes almost black in colour. There is discomfort in the region of the stomach with severe pain over the liver and the spleen is enlarged. The fever rises to one hundred and four degrees or higher. The urine becomes scanty and finally may be suppressed altogether. When this happens the prospect of recovery is slim indeed.

Mild cases recover in a few days, providing as soon as the temperature rises, the patient is put to bed. It is a mistake to go about as ususal, and especially dangerous to travel. But in severe infections the patient becomes progressively anemic and may die from this or from heart failure. Death may also be caused by kidney failure due to damage of the kidney by the blood pigment in the urine. Relapses may occur, with the tendency of it leading to a second attack. The third is usually fatal. But individuals may survive many atacks. Doctors state that after two attacks it is inadvisable to return to the tropics.

When I came down with a high fever back in October, I treated it as benign malaria, the common form which I have had countless times throughout the years. Took the usual dosage of chloroquine and awaited recovery. But the hot bath does not break the fever this time as it had done on previous occasions. Instead it worsened matters. My temperature shot up and I almost succumbed. Just made it back into bed, my heart doing it's best to keep beating.

My urine turned darker and darker. It is then that we

realized I had blackwater fever, the disease fatal to so many whites only decades ago. My recovery had been painfully slow. There were times when my weakened heart wanted to call it quits. I begged the Lord to keep it going. I wanted to see the kids once more. I got so homesick for them away out there in Canada. I wanted them to know I loved them and wished the best for them. "Please Lord," I had prayed, "Get me on my feet again so that we can all be together once more while in Africa." All our children are coming to see us this summer.

The Lord had heard my prayers. I had recovered but it had left me exhausted for weeks, and my mouth covered with fever blisters. Now here I am coming down with blackwater fever again. I dreaded it. It was not going to be pleasant.

Have a restless night again. Hear some shooting and screaming not far away. I feel weak and still have a fever. My temperature stays over one hundred and three degrees. No appetite. I force myself to gulp down the juices and broth Marion concocts for me. It is becoming more difficult to pass my urine which is foul smelling . Took all the will power I had the last time round. My temperature by evening is over one hundred and four degrees.

At six that evening Rufus appears at the gate just as I am dressing to go and get examined by a doctor. Return to bed instead and have him and Marion lay on hands and pray for me. Tomorrow he and I were to start on our ten-day safari which would take us to Teso, Bugisu and Bukedi districts. But now he will have to go alone and do as much as he is able. There still is no power which went off this afternoon when we turn in for the night. There is much shooting tonight, the most I have heard for a long time! Most of it is coming from below us.

My high fever broke around two, so I feel better this morning. Weak though with burning in my bladder. Marion takes Rufus to the bus park and picks up the mail. The power comes back on just before noon. Begin eating solids after only liquids for two days. My temperature wavers around one hundred and one degrees throughout the afternoon. Up a lot due to company. Too much. There is pain in my temples and behind my eyes tonight. A couple of shots nearby, the rest distant. Cannot sleep until midnight. Thinking a lot of the kids.

Wake up to a clear Sunday morning. Marion goes to the service at Kasubi taking along the four workers. I do not feel too bad, but need to keep off the roads, especially these in Kampala. While they are gone I write a letter to Colleen and get ready a birthday card for Mark. He will be twenty in two weeks. Sat around in the afternoon with company. Go to bed tonight drained and exhausted. There is pressure in my upper stomach region. The liver and spleen are still swollen.

Up at six this morning. Re-writing what I had jotted down during the night plus adding something here and there to it. For at two o'clock the Holy Spirit moved on me to start writing my books of experiences I have had as a missionary in East Africa. So I had gotten up and commenced putting down some thoughts. This finally might be the beginnings of what has been my goal for years. Share it with Marion and she feels good about it.

I work on my writings throughout the day. We retire early tonight. When weighing myself, I find I have lost fifteen pounds during my bout with blackwater fever! May it not happen again is my prayer.

# Chapter Nine
# The Coup

"Army Mutiny in Uganda" read the headlines in one of Kenya's leading newspapers, the Standard, while the Nation blares "Ugandan Rebels Cut off Two Regions." This is Friday, July 26, 1985. We are in Kisumu, Kenya, loading supplies before heading on to Uganda. With Marion and I are our son Mark and daughter Colleen with her husband Tim. Our other son Kirk with his wife Karen, we left back in Nairobi in consultation with World Vision International for assignment to the Sudan. Mark came out for his summer holiday and has been with us for two months while Colleen and Tim arrived a few weeks ago.

What are we returning to in Uganda? And our children are with us! Things have been happening quickly in the past two weeks. Besides the nightly gunfire, explosions were rocking the city of Kampala before we left for our vacation in Kenya two weeks ago. And now there is a mutiny in the main army! It has been tough enough with the various guerrilla forces stationed throughout the Uganda bush.

As we enter Uganda, the Custom's officer says, "So you've come back!" Is he surprised to see me return to his troubled land? Along the route to Kampala we meet the regular roadblocks, some of them are manned by soldiers and others by the police. We are allowed to continue without any request for identification. Reaching home the watchmen inform us that there has been shooting during the nights we have been gone. That isn't really anything new here in Kampala. We give thanks to our Lord for His wonderous protection of lives and possession during our absence before we commence unloading our stuff.

Saturday forenoon I take Tim with me to town for some shopping. Mark remains with his mother and Colleen who are washing clothes. After picking up the mail we tackle the market. While carrying the purchased fruits and vegetables to the vehicle several people run by me. Are they chasing a thief? I've seen that happen before so I push on to the vehicle where Tim is waiting.

Soon more are running, all in the same direction. Then vehicles begin pulling away from the market. I ask a passerby, "What is happening?" He replies that soldiers are entering the city on Bombo Road which links up with Kampala Road. It is now eleven in the morning. I do not join the mad exodus as I have heard of previous raids by undisciplined soldiers. They come to loot some shops and then retreat to their barracks. Surely they won't attack the market which is below the main thoroughfare of town!

Across from the market shopkeepers are locking up their premises. A V.W. bug speeds by containing two pale and frightened European nuns. The vehicle wasn't travelling fast enough for them. Tim and I watch the street and market place emptying itself rapidly of pedestrians and vehicles. It is as though they are being spewed out from before our eyes. There is fear in the air.

The little urchin who had carried my basket asks me, "What are you waiting for?" I reply, "Why?" He says, "They will kill everyone." It is then that Tim and I climb into the Nissan, swing it around just as a landcruiser flies by almost hitting us and we make our way to Entebbe Road, a block from here. Arriving we find traffic spilling onto it from Kampala Road. At the junction a motorist stops in front of us, climbs out and looks around at all the confusion. He must have just arrived and hadn't yet heard what was happening. It's only for a moment though. He hurriedly ducks back inside and joins the cavalcade exiting Kampala. It didn't take him long to catch on!

On Entebbe Road the whole street is one-way traffic right now. Tim and I are moving along rapidly bumper to bumper and with vehicles on either side, close enough to shake the driver's hand as well as the passenger without a problem. The cars on my left are in actuality off the street and driving on what is supposed to be for pedestrians who are sprinting madly, weaving in and out of the traffic. Panic is on the faces of many! Those who are carrying loads on their heads now drop them.

In spite of all this, there are a few drivers who smile back at us when we glance their way as we race along. Going by some parked vehicles we notice a man jump out of one of them and start running. Then he stops and dashes back. Must have forgotten his briefcase. No, all he does is slam the door shut which he had left ajar, and then he's off again. Is that all? When excited we do some funny things.

At the clock tower round-about more traffic converges into Entebbe Road. It's now a mass of vehicles everywhere! Nearly drive over a lady who trips as she darts in front of me. I wave her on as I decrease the speed giving her enough time to collect her wits. The panic now is high-pitched, and we are caught in the middle of it!

Before turning left onto Gaba Road which leads to Muyenga, we spot a lone European lady jammed in the fleeing mob. Catching her eye I motion if she wants a lift. She forces her way out of the crowd and over to where I have slowed down as much as possible without causing a collision. She hits the door before Tim can open it.

Rifle fire is now splitting the air. They sound like electric sparks. Driving now parallel to main Kampala we hear heavier weapons join the fracus. I have the funny urge to duck each time there is an outburst. Must be because Tim has his window rolled down which is the side facing the city. A lot of help a pane of glass would do should bullets come our way!

Dust churns up as vehicles, including ours, pass over the broken stretch of road leading across the tracks. The many pot-holes aren't slowing down anyone. Pull in at the Total petrol station where I usually fill up and find it locked and vacated. My fuel guage registers nearly empty. Should have heeded the tug I had to fill up earlier when on my way to town. Too late now. So much for leaving things to the last.

We stop at Kabalagala, a small center at the foot of our hill. I didn't quite finish my shopping at the market back in town so I need to do it here. But I find all the vendors have gone! Their produce is still there, only no one to serve me. At the meat stall I cannot locate a knife to cut off several kilos. I know the owner and intend to pay the next time I see him. Someone else wanting meat joins me but he too is unable to help himself. Maybe he finally did as I leave him there. Need to get on home. (This market was looted of everything in it not much later.)

Before going home we take the lady we had picked up at the round-about on to a place where she has some friends. We traverse a side road to get there. Bombs are exploding in town as we pull into our yard. The women are relieved to see us home safe. Marion says that Colleen had started to cry, "Mom, Tim and dad are down there!", when the shooting had started. They witnessed the exodus of vehicles from Kampala flooding Gaba Road.

We sit on our front veranda and watch the fall of Kampala. It doesn't fall into the hands of Museveni and his guerrilla force but to the mutinying army of President Obote. At twelve thirty in the afternoon Radio Uganda comes on the air after a long silence. Okello, the army commander announces that the government has been toppled.

Gunfire continues throughout the afternoon. There are bombs as well as artillery and mortar fire echoing among the hills of greater Kampala. A crowd has lined up along Gaba Road. They wish to cheer the victors which they know will soon be coming to take up posts at all road junctions. And they don't have long to wait. We see their waving and hear their shouting as the troops roll by them. A space of only a few hours ago that same crowd had been fleeing frantically for cover. Now they are rejoicing. Truly, there is a time to rejoice and a time to refrain from rejoicing.

There were bombs and sporadic gunfire all night. It doesn't stop but carries on after daybreak. Smoke can be seen coming from the center of the city. Now the looting begins. We witness soldiers, whether they are of Obote or of Okello we are not sure, commandeer vehicles travelling on Tank Hill Road. The owner and his passengers are ordered out and the new occupants speed away with headlights blinking. This happens over and over to the unsuspecting motorists who turn the corner to climb the hill.

Over in the industrial area warehouses are being raided. Hundreds file away transporting loads of loot on their heads. On our hill we now notice owners hiding their Mercedes Benz behind buildings in isolated areas. We are up higher and their movements are visible to us.

It is eleven o'clock and we prepare ourselves for a time of worship in our living room. The workers join us. A rifle shot cracks loudly almost at our door! It startles everyone of us. It comes as a total surprise.

A pickup containing soldiers had just passed our gate and then stopped at the next house which is just across the hedge from us. It is there that they fired the shot and were now ordering the man to bring the keys to his vehicles and all the cash he has inside. One knocks him down with his rifle butt when resistance is shown. He is held down with a well placed boot on his neck until the keys and money are produced by the family. They speed away with two of his Mercedes Benz and the cardboard box full of bank notes.

What are we doing all this time? While Patrick, one of our watchmen, is peeking through the hedge observing all that is taking place next door we are singing hymns. Mind you it starts off rather shakily but we soon gain momento. The hymns Marion picked to begin with are too sobering—"In the Sweet Bye and Bye" and "When We All Get to Heaven." But the Word which I read from John 17 and Psalm 91 renews us and strengthens our wobbly knees. Praise the Lord!

While dozing in the afternoon I can faintly hear someone saying, "There are soldiers at the gate!" Marion soon has me fully awake when she says, "Stan, get up! Soldiers are at the gate!" I jump up and by the time I get down the steps, Tim is talking to them. I hear one saying to him, "Aren't you frightened?" Tim replies, "Not yet."

There are three Europeans, one of them a woman, with the two soldiers. The woman keeps telling us not to open the gate, she only wants some directions from me. She's looking for a house of a friend and the soldiers are escorting her in her own car. I am able to point it out to her and send Patrick along to make sure they get there. Before they leave, the one who says he is Captain Apoliano warns us to stay inside the compound and not venture out for a week. He adds that he is coming back for one of our watchdogs when they are older.

Our evening meal we spend out on the patio. Today is Colleen and Tim's sixth wedding anniversary! No frills but it is the best we can do under the circumstances. Occasional gunfire intersperses our time of celebrating.

Monday morning and it has quieted down after a night of much shooting. There has been no running water since Saturday which means our storage tanks are nigh empty. It is decided to set up an outdoor latrine over the man-hole cover of our septic tank. This should save on our meager water supply. And, no more showers or baths! Only with the sponge.

Mid afternoon we discover people helping themselves to diesel from a stranded tanker down at the Kabalagala crossroad. I need some myself. I send Patrick to investigate. He reports back that someone is selling it by the jerry can. Soon three of our jerry cans are on their way down the hill. Francis our second watchman accompanies Patrick. Plus Francis Makosia, our evangelist in eastern region, who gets caught visiting us when the coup takes place. As the three approach the tanker a Landrover full of soldiers pulls up alongside. Both Francises know enough to duck behind some shops with their jerry cans to await the outcome of Patrick's attempt to fetch diesel.

We watch Patrick leave the huddle of soldiers. He is without the jerry can! They come back up the hill swinging two empty jerry cans. And minus some money. The soldiers had waited until he had paid for the fuel before ordering him to stick the can in their vehicle.

Later on in the afternoon Tim, Mark, and I venture out on foot to visit a missionary couple who live around the corner at the bottom of the hill. A telephone call had come through from Nairobi enquiring as to their welfare. We pass the residence for International Red Cross personnel where one of them informs us that thirty of their vehicles have already been stolen.

Reaching the road at the bottom we come upon some onlookers beside the road. At their feet lying in the grass is a man his side covered in blood. I notice he is still breathing faintly inspite of being shot several times. I ask the bystander whether someone had gone for help. I knew as soon as I asked that they had not. It was a dumb thing to say anyway. What did they care whether one more died. Didn't so many die that no one was counting them in the last few days? But I go on to tell them that the Red Cross is just above and someone should notify them. They will make sure he gets to a doctor.

Walking away I feel terrible that we were unable to help the man ourselves. We are on foot. If the Red Cross was losing their vehicles, what about ours? We only have the one. What can we do? The man will not live. Not even another statistic!

We find the missionary couple safe and give them the message from Nairobi. Then we start for home. We meet an International Red Cross vehicle on this back road and inform them of the dying man. What a coincidence! Or is it an answer to prayer? They assure us that they will pick him up. Before we reach our place we come across a black Mercedes being stripped right there on the trail. The two grin at us as we move past them. A happy lot these thieves! They may have even posed for us had we brought along a camera.

Kima Mission calls us tonight to see how we are faring. We are unable to call out as no operator is on duty since the coup took place. Direct dialing to reach us from the outside is possible. But for us we are able to dial direct to Nairobi only. So we are waiting for our friends to ring us as we are unable to notify them of our safety.

Before retiring tonight we watch the tracer bullets from the veranda arching across the sky. Their red glow fizzling out before they land. Where do they land anyway? Much shooting below us. Looters are on the prowl and no one to defend the public. We hear women ululating not far to our right. It is a high pitched yodel. They are broadcasting, to whoever is intererested and willing to help, that their homes are being attacked by gunmen.

When morning comes it is quiet. Then mid afternoon we begin receiving water. The workmen busy themselves washing their clothes. Our outdoor latrine is dismantled. Mark finds a spent bullet lying on our driveway in front of the garage. I was wondering yesterday where all the bullets shot into the air went. Here is one of them!

At four in the afternoon we receive a call from the Canadian High Commission in Nairobi. They inform us that there will be an evacuation of the European population and advises us to join the convoy which is leaving for Kenya tomorrow morning. Well, it has come to this!

The British and Americans have decided to evacuate their subjects. I think we have come through the worst of it so why leave now? But then we did plan to leave in a few more days anyway. We have a safari planned before Mark's departure for Canada which will take us to our old stamping grounds in Tanzania. So why not leave a few days earlier? The borders are closed and so is the international airport. Who knows when they will open. We decide to join the exodus tomorrow.

Before we can leave though we need fuel. The boys and I back out the Nissan from the garage where it has been locked since Saturday and drive cautiously down the road to town. Pass a crowd viewing a corpse in the ditch. No one has claimed it yet. Find the Total filling station looted. Shelves are bare, pumps overturned or leaning precariously. We pass two more stations before we find one which has diesel. Upon paying him I ask for a receipt. He says to return tomorrow for it as he cannot assist me with one today. We have a good laugh and pull away. I am fortunate to have gotten fuel! Why ask for a receipt? Someone had gotten killed while he was waiting for his receipt at a petrol station in southwest Africa a short time ago.

Driving through the city we find it deserted except for soldiers squatting on the sidewalks at different points. Shops are empty. Many windows are broken and others have bullet holes sprayed across them. An anti-aircraft gun is sitting at the intersection of Entebbe and Kampala Roads. A soldier is in the seat manning it while others are loitering nearby. We see two more after this as we take the road past Crested Towers. I suppose they use them mainly for shelling hillsides as there are no planes to shoot at, only a few helicopters. Several roadblocks along the route but they do not stop us. They are

friendly and wave back at us. Many of them just youngsters.

In the morning we give the workers food and money
enough to last until our return. Then we have prayer
with them before departing for the British High Commission down town. Enroute we stop at the anti-aircraft
gun which stands near the intersection. Mark wants
some of the empty shells. He is given a handful by the
accommodating soldiers. Many vehicles are already standing in line when we pull up at the British High Commission building. The American Embassy is just next
door.

The first convoy of cars leaves at nine. Then an hour
later we are on the road in a convoy of fifteen vehicles
with a British official in the lead. The British Military
(B.M.A.T.T.) is in charge of this operation and are doing
a marvelous job. They must have had previous evacuation exercises as they seem to be enjoying the lamplight.
Just past Jinja the convoy is halted for a tea break. We
pull into Busia by the border at four in the afternoon.

After waiting in line for two hours we are told that no
vehicles are permitted to leave Uganda. Only the passengers are free to cross. Apparently the border officials
on the Uganda side are still awaiting instructions from
Kampala. The British officer says if I wish to stay with
the vehicle I may do so to await any further developments tomorrow.

Say goodbye to Marion and the kids. I watch them
carry their luggage across the border into Kenya. When
will I see them again? Buses are waiting on the other
side to transport the evacuees to Kisumu or Nairobi
after formalities have been completed with Kenyan officials.

I swing the vehicle around and park it alongside others

on an empty lot a short distance from the gate leading to Kenya. I begin thinking about where I will meet the family again. The whole thing is up in the air! I could not accompany them as someone has to stay with the vehicle. Otherwise it surely will get stolen. The parting was too rushed. When we learned that they could cross, and then immediately due to the lateness of the hour, we only had time to say our farewell. There was no, "See you at such-and such a place at such-and-such a time!"

Sitting there pondering these thoughts as the sun is sinking, out of sight, Tim appears out of nowhere! Brings me news that Marion has been able to call Kima Mission and that Paul Hutchins is now coming for them. They will be waiting for me at Kima. What a relief! Thank God they will be alright now.

Tonight I, along with others, gather around the B.M.A.T.T. lorry and we are given rations. While there I learn that one hundred and fifty vehicles containing six hundred occupants had left Kampala today. I count just over one hundred vehicles parked here for the night awaiting tomorrow's decision. The rest have returned to Kampala or gone somewhere else after discovering they could not cross into Kenya.

Several of us contribute money towards the purchasing of two goats. We roast them over an open fire in the center of the court. Vehicles have been parked, facing inwards, in a large circle on the advice of the army to discourage thieving. The British seem to be able to rise to these occasions and make sport of such incidents.

Slept well in the back of my Nissan. Christians from the Busia church bring me breakfast this morning. Francis Makosia was with us in the convoy yesterday and has informed our people here of past events. They are very sympathetic of our plight and Francis leads in prayer before parting.

It is forenoon when the B.M.A.T.T. commander asks us to line up our vehicles at the border gate. Permission has been granted by the Ugandan authorities to take them across. But we are to hurry before they change their minds. It is an anxious moment when the official looks at my log-book. Will he ask for a bond? Someone has mentioned they are requiring on amounting into quite a sum. I do not have that much on me. But he waves me through after I sign their book. Praise the Lord! I am in Kenya where there is none of this. An hour later I pull into Kima and am reunited with my wife, Colleen, Tim and Mark. the strain of separation is over at last!

# Chapter Ten
# And There Shall Be Wars

Uganda has been a war-torn country ever since one cares to remember. Before and after the turn of the twentieth century there was fighting between tribes and kingdoms. Only during the colonial years was there a lull on the battlefield. But it did not take long once the Union Jack had been lowered for its last time for the fighting to resume.

Is this their lot? To be shedding blood constantly? There are so many wonderful people in this marvellous country which is being devastated inch by inch. Its beauty, so tarnished that only nature and God can ever restore it to its former glory. And they could, if given time and a chance.

Could a reason be, why the land is still crying and God remaining silent, that some of her wonderful people know they are wonderful? And are proud of it? "Pride goes before destruction, and a haughty spirit before a fall," reads Proverbs 16:18. In spite of all the suffering that has taken place in recent times, it has not devastated them. The proud continue to be proud and the haughty continue to be as haughty as ever. When will they humble themselves for it is only then that wars ease. "If any people who are called by my name *humble themselves* and pray, and seek my face and *turn from their wicked ways,* then I will hear from heaven, *will forgive their sin,* and *will heal their land"* (2 Chronicles 7:14).

After the military coup which ousted Milton Obote, the new head of state Tito Okello tries to bring in all the guerilla factions from the bush to form a new ruling council until such a time elections can be held. In the months that follow five of the six unite themselves with the U.N.L.A. except for one which is the largest and strongest, the N.R.A. under Museveni. He keeps insisting there is no big difference between what there has been and what there is now. So he still means to topple the government and install his own.

Finally in December, a peace agreement is signed between the two opposing forces in Nairobi, for which the Kenyan president Moi has worked so hard to bring to pass. The Ugandans rejoice! All except those who still want to settle matters on the battlefield. One month later fighting resumes. And the peace accord gradually becomes only a piece of paper.

By this time the N.R.A. has crept into all of southwest Uganda, occupying one-third of the country. They are now preparing to take the capital, Kampala. The long awaited day is about to dawn. How big a battle will it be? Will Museveni's forces take it? Or will he be repulsed? How safe are we here at Muyenga on the outskirts of the city?

We are no longer able to travel to our Kigezi and Ankole churches which are in the southwest as the N.R.A. closed the road in August, a month after the coup. As well, the road to our Bunyoro churches in the mid-west has become too dangerous to traverse due to clashes between the two forces. This leaves only one safe route out of the city. And that is to the east, which leads to Jinja, and eventually the border with Kenya or up to Mbale and then on around Lake Kyoga which straddles central Uganda.

Because of these circumstances, we spend much time with our eastern churches in Samia, Bugisu, Bukedi and Teso. We even open churches in Busoga. As well, a safari is made, when it becomes safe enough, to our Lango churches in the north. During and right after the coup, many atrocities had taken place here in Obote's tribe. It is heart rending as we listen to account after account of brutality and savagery committed by the army that swept through.

Besides stealing their livestock, they set ablaze their houses, grain bins and crops. Women are raped, pregnant mothers slit open, girls carried away, infants smashed to death, and men horribly tortured before being killed. At times the grain was spilled in the center of the room, then urinated upon and excretion mixed into it. The same would be done with books and similar items. Many of our people had run into the bush taking with them all they could carry. There they waited and prayed until it was safe to return.

I make plans to go up to the West Nile and visit our churches in Alur. With the signing of the peace treaty it should be safe enough. Have not been up there for over six months. The last seminar had to be cancelled due to the fighting which continued in that direction after the coup. Rufus is to go there ahead of me, traveling the northern route, picking up Wilson along the way to assist him. We finalize the details during a weekend seminar in Busia.

Unknown to Rufus and me as we are making plans for the West Nile, Museveni is making plans to seize Kampala which will strand Rufus and Wilson behind the battle line for weeks without our knowledge of their whereabouts or welfare.

The N.R.A. arrive on the outskirts and commence shelling on Friday, the 17th of January, 1986, the day I begin the seminar at Busia for the Samia church leaders. But I do not know it. The B.B.C. and the Voice of America have been covering quite well the situation in Uganda, but I have not been listening to the radio since my arrival here. When the seminar ends on Sunday, someone comes up with a Kenyan newspaper, the Nation, which has the headlines—"Fighting Rages around Kampala!"

In the morning I cross over into Kenya and do some shopping in Kisumu seventy-five miles away. We are able to purchase supplies here for one-third the price it is in Kampala. Today's newspaper headlines—"Thousands Flee Kampala Gunfire!"

I ring Marion and ask how bad things are. Yes, there is fighting at Natete, a suburb of Kampala. They can hear a lot of shooting including the big guns. Refugees are fleeing from the troubled area. A lady running for her life came to the house on Saturday for help. She lost her husband and four family members in the fighting at Natete. She was fed and kept the night, then her fare paid to Jinja where her parents reside. And, oh yes, she adds "Load up with supplies!" I hang up with a heavy heart. Why can there not be peace in Uganda?

I arrive back home without a mishap. Several of the road-blocks wanted to know what I carried but nothing serious. I expected any time I may have to run a gauntlet of gunfire. But the closest I came to any real sign of the war is the movement of troops towards the capital. Get caught behind a large tank and no one is allowed to pass it. Armored vehicles, one on either side of it, are escorting it. For miles we crawl along behind it until we reach proper Kampala where they turn into a side street. I find Marion, as well as Colleen and Tim cheerful and braced for what ever happens.

It is a coincidence that our daughter and her husband should be present for another war! They were here for their holidays when the coup took place, and now they are here as missionaries on special assignment when there is fighting again in Kampala. They arrived just two weeks ago to our fair city. Uganda is going to turn them into war veterans!

On Tuesday we listen to heavy guns all forenoon. They come from the direction of Katete. It quiets down in the evening. It resumes Wednesday morning plus there is bombing. Gunships (helicopters) are being used by the government troops against the guerrilla forces to try and halt them. Museveni's troops are coming in on two fronts as there are now big guns booming to the north besides those in the west.

I decide we need more supplies and head for town, Tim accompaning me. We meet Elijah, our pastor at Kasubi, near the post office. He informs us that all his neighbors have fled as there is fighting nearby. It is becoming unsafe he says as government soldiers are looting and raping. Could we come after four and move them over to our compound? I consent to his request. But we end up going there sooner when we notice hundreds of people and vehicle after vehicle streaming down the road towards Kabalagala at the foot of our hill. Heavy guns are again barking after a short lull.

Tim and I wend our way back into the city. Kasubi lies

directly across town from us. The capital is engulfed in panic! Thousands are fleeing for their lives on foot. We meet many lorries jammed with troops. The fighting must be spilling over into the city center!

The troops quickly take to robbing people of money, watches, and anything they can get a hold of easily. They also break into shops and loot property. We reach Kasubi safely. The surrounding houses are deserted except for a prowling dog and a half naked kid dashing round a corner. We commence packing their belongings into the back of the Nissan. Besides all the stuff they plan to take I must leave enough space for ten people, not counting Tim and myself. Elijah is remaining behind and plans to come tomorrow. I hurry them along when they keep returning for more. A helicopter sweeps by us hugging the tree-tops. It is one of the government gunships.

Finally we are moving. Discover the streets are now empty. Kampala has become a ghost town! We dash down the deserted thoroughfare. Ahead of us is a roadblock. An empty Landrover is to one side while soldiers are busily ushering a man out of his white car in front of me. We are motioned to stop. Expecting an immediate wave on as with previous occasions, I am startled to hear one of them bark, "Toka!" ("Get out!") I begin slowly to pull the Nissan over to the side of the street. The soldier misinterpreting my move, barks out again the same command, "Toka!" Tim leans out the window and says, "We will, we will" in Swahili. The children behind me stare wide-eyed.

During this time many government troops have begun to desert, realizing they cannot crush the guerrilla forces which keep advancing regardless of what they do. Rampaging soldiers are commandeering vehicles and fleeing east to Jinja. Am I going to lose my vehicle to this frightened lot?

Preparing to step out after opening my door, I look across to the soldiers on my side who are busy with the white car. The officer there just then looks up and seeing who I am, and the name on the door now facing him, tells me to proceed! I nod my thanks and proceed on home. Praise God for that soldier! There must be many more like him who will die needlessly before this war is over.

This evening there is plenty of shooting near us. A bullet whizzes by Marion and Tim as they chat on the front veranda! People scurry to and fro with belongings on their heads. We go to bed to the sound of big guns booming into the night air. "Lord, we rest 'neath your everlasting arms where no ill can befall us. Amen."

All is still when we awaken in the morning. By mid morning there is some traffic. Colleen has an appointment for a prenatal check-up at Nsambya Hospital. Tim drives her over at eleven o'clock. It is between here and town. Not a conducive atmosphere for an expectant mother! They find the Sister too busy due to the casualties of the war. There are many soldiers about.

Elijah shows up and reports that the city center is dead. There is no public transportation so he walked all the way. Most vehicles moving were carrying armed soldiers with very few civilian motorists. He survived the night at Kasubi without an incident. We now have nineteen on our compound watching the battle for the capital. How long will it last? One day more? A week? The coup last July came abruptly and ended quickly. What about this time? Will we have enough food to feed all of us?

The warden on the hill drops in and warns us to stay

inside and not wander out of the compound especially with the vehicle as soldiers are taking them from civilians. Elijah attempts to return to Kasubi in the afternoon but fails. The army has the road blocked off at Nsambya. As darkness falls and the shooting erupts again we all gather on our terraced lawn over-looking the siezed city and pray for safety through the night. Outside our gate just across the lane are the two hundred or so refugees who will be spending the night again on the ground. They were there last night too. Protect them once more, Lord.

We have not heard so much cannon and rocket fire since the coup as we do around midnight! Before sunrise there is a lull in the fighting. Then only sporadic shooting until noon. But after that it gains momento and the fighting becomes intense from then on. It is an all out battle for the control of Kampala! The city is now the battleground. The N.R.A. troops entered the southern part of Kampala last night and are stationed on Rubaga hill near the Roman Catholic cathedral. They also entered Kampala via Kabalagala this morning from the east, after arriving by boat on Lake Victoria.

Radio Uganda goes off the air at one fifteen in the afternoon. We can hear heavy gunfire everywhere! The ammunition dump at Lubiri barracks, Kampala's biggest army garrison, is hit by a shell and huge clouds of smoke bellow upwards. Explosions continue for over an hour. The big gun on Kololo hill must have been put out of commission by the guerrillas this afternoon as it has fallen silent.

A lot of shooting here at Tank Hill now. It is fortunate that Tim and Elijah went when they did this morning to Kabalagala for beans, to add to our larder. It is a battleground down there now. Soldiers are everywhere. One was hit by a sniper at the junction. After a few attempts we see him drag himself off the road.

We busy ourselves by answering several letters. My head is throbbing from all the heavy gunfire today. Many of those who fled Nsambya, following a bomb explosion which killed many and injured others, are camped outside our gate. We feed them mangoes from our tree.

Nothing is afoot to evacuate foreigners. I would think it is more dangerous to try to move than to sit tight right now. Everyone is staying home and waiting to see what happens. Besides, it is a lawless state right now. No one is in charge here in the capital. "Continue to set your angels to guard us Lord! You are all we have got to help us."

Sunrise! A beautiful Saturday morning. The birds are singing in spite of the shooting which has resumed. We heard heavy gunfire until three o'clock last night. There is no water so the outdoor latrine is assembled once more as we did during the coup. Power goes off as well around ten o-clock. That makes it three out of three! No phone, no water and no power!

Several buildings are hit down town. One of them is the Treasury Branch. Fire destroys the roof completely. Makindyi barracks on the ridge across from us is attacked. They shell it continuously. There are skirmishes at Kabalagala and also right below us on the side of the hill. Bullets whistle near us several times. We note soldiers ducking through gardens and over hedges.

While visiting on our front veranda with missionary friends who have walked over to greet us, bullets fly in our direction! They pass through the bougenvillia beside us, one goes through a flower pot, three glance off the patio floor and another one hits the side of the house!

We duck and scramble inside. That is too close!

Why did the soldiers patrolling the road below shoot at us? Did it have something to do with their commander who was passing in front of us just at that time on his way to the hotel he is staying at? He has been moving with his vehicle back and forth a lot. Rumors have it that he, Kayira, will be joining forces with Museveni.

Thousands of government troops are fleeing towards Jinja. Many are on foot, we notice through our binoculars, and others jammed in vehicles or on top of lorries. The gunfire dies down finally this evening. Columns of people are winding their way along pathways to places of safety for the night. Each one is carrying something on his or her head. We hand out mangoes to those who come to the gate.

We retire early. The pressure lamp is making too much noise. It is better without it. Need to be able to hear. And it is not long before we do hear shouting and ululating. It is away down in the city. We get up and sit on our front veranda to listen to what appears to be a celebration. It is ten o'clock and still no electricity anywhere. But they have some kind of light down there. Probably burning torches made from grass as it is giving forth a red glow. Must have lighted tires as well along the walkway. We are guessing that it is Museveni making his triumphant entry! Kampala is now his after a nine day offensive of the city.

Then we notice residents of our hill racing down to join those at Kabalagala in the celebrations. They are cheering, whooping and ululating. Above all this rejoicing big guns boom sporadically with plenty of automatic firing. Bullets whiz by us! Others arch through the darkness, tiny red glows streaming in different directions including ours.

Sunday morning there is a brief shoot-out below us and then it is calm. At ten o'clock the power comes on, just in time for our service here in the house. Elijah delivers the messge after Marion has shown us biblical filmstrips. No interruptions this time, as during the coup.

Late afternoon Tim and I transport Elijah and his crew back to Kasubi. He is anxious to check his premises, how it weathered the war. Many dead liter the streets and round-a-bouts. Some have already had parts of their wearing apparel removed. At the post office where numerous soldiers patrolled, lie their bodies now scattered about. A few road-blocks but their attendants are easy going. Young men from Museveni's tribe.

At Kasubi, we find the inhabitants are gradually returning to their homes. Elijah's place has not been touched. Praise the Lord! We return to Muyenga without a mishap. Spot one other European on the road driving his vehicle.

All night the city remains dark. It is silent at Makindyi barracks this morning. But big guns had been going off in that direction since yesterday evening. Then we see why. Down the ridge swarm about six hundred soldiers who have surrendered. Dis-arming continues as N.R.A. troops round up fugitive army soldiers. The water starts running finally.

By afternoon our phone is still not functioning, so Tim and I drive down to the post office to use theirs. We discover it is still closed, as well as all the shops and businesses. N.R.A. soldiers are everywhere. Civilians are strolling about and the dead of yesterday have been removed. The remains of a tank and lorry collision blocks one street near the Parliament building which is pox-marked with bullet holes. Most buildings, we note, are thus decorated. Even the Bible Society shop was shot at, its large window smashed.

Before returning home, we enter Lubiri barracks. A friendly soldier escorts us around. There are still dead bodies lying around. They were full of life and held a gun only a couple of days ago. Now they are lifeless, their hands empty. Jesus said, "All those who take up the sword shall perish by the sword!" (Matthew 26:52). In this case it was the rifle.

Tuesday morning, we pray that God will help the phone to work as we need to notify our relatives of our safety. God answers our prayer! It begins to function by nine o'clock. We ring up Marion's mother and she is overjoyed at hearing our voices. She tells us she had just been praying that she would hear from us that very evening. (It is ten o'clock in the evening there now!) The phone had to work with prayers going up at both ends. God answers her prayer as well.

Before hanging up, we ask her to inform Mark that we are well. Our son is at college in Alberta and very difficult to reach. Kirk and Karen are in Sudan, so I send them a telex through Lifeline in Nairobi. Am informed they have one for us from the children enquiring how we are. No sooner had I made these two calls when the phone goes dead!

(top)
Author and his wife
(middle)
Bullets whistled by
as we watched from
our veranda.
(bottom)
Muyenga Hill
and Gaba Road

Clock tower on Entebbe Road, Kampala.

Purchasing fish at Kabalagala market.

Cattle foraging at a market dump.

Kinyonga church built in memory of Marion's dad.

Seeking God's help at the altar.

On the road again.

We must toil and plant before we can reap.

While the meal is being prepared there is time for a shave and a shower.

Docking at an island in Lake Victoria.

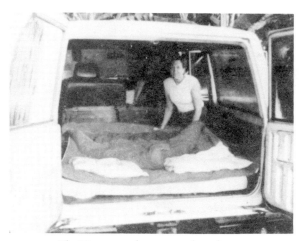

The Nissan, our home away from home.

Bibles and books for our T.E.E. program.

John, Godfrey, Francis, Elijah, Ephraim, Wilson, and Arthur—
T.E.E. graduates and their certificates.

A congregation meeting under a tree.

This congregation has started on its building.

Relief for an area hit by Karamojong raiders.

They litter the countryside in the Luwero Triangle.

A converted policeman.

A casualty in one of the wars.

A view from our front door—the shelling of Kampala.

One of the bullets that missed us went through the flower pot.

Bombed out building in downtown Kampala.

Ignatius beaten
while in prison.

With his "toto"
(child)—an AK-47.

One of our Christian soldiers.

(top)
Soldiers waiting
at roadblock.

(middle)
A boy soldier
in the N.R.A.

Passengers being
checked at roadblock.

(bottom)
A witchdoctor who
accepted Christ.

(above) Marion treating the sick.

(above right) Teaching the women.

Lame man healed.

(above) Colleen busy with
correspondence and reports.

(right) Paulo, with his church,
survived the Idi Amin era.

Rufus and Wilson after their 185-mile trek to safety through the war zone.

It is the season for the "Kumbu-Kumbu" (flying ants) here prepared in three different ways.

Candidates for circumcision.

The procession.

The initiation.

Time for the elders to sip beer.

(left) Francis with the Karamojong.
(right) Karamojong women.

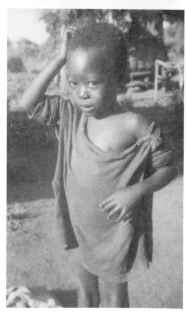

(left) with Karamojong elders.
(right) In need of brotherly love.

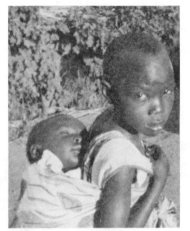

Baby-sitters, with or without clothes.

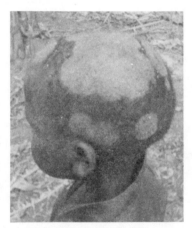

(left) Healed after he surrendered his demon-infested grove. (middle) Ringworm has eaten away most of his hair. (right) Mother snatched from death through prayer.

Pupils using the ground in a bush school.

Tim commencing to build Kasubi Day Care Centre.

Now 80 tots keep Colleen busy in these facilities.

Dad, Mom, Tim, Colleen, Mark, Karen, Kirk.

The Stevensons.

Tiffany with
her mother,
grandmother,
and great-
grandmother!

(left) Basuti,
the Baganda
dress for
married women.

Three different musical instruments.

A vision for the regions beyond.
(left) Baptizing the converts.

Helping me with my last chapter.

"How is this, Grandpa?"

To Tiffany with love.

# Chapter Eleven
## Cut-Off

It is less than a week since the capture of Kampala by the National Resistance Army (N.R.A.) and we are wondering whether it is safe enough to venture up to Kinyonga for the scheduled seminar this weekend. We have heard that Bombo Road, the route we always take, is unsafe. The fleeing troops of the previous army are still using it to reach Acholi to the north.

Enquiring at the bus park, I was advised to use the road to Hoima. Once there, swing right and head for Kigumba via Masindi. So that is what we will do. It will mean travelling one hundred kilometers further this time.

We manage to leave mid-forenoon after committing ourselves to Him in prayer. Colleen and Tim are remaining behind. The road we are on has seen very little travel during the past six years. The grass is tall on either side of it. In places it resembles only a trail. There are rough and very dusty sections as well.

The villages we pass through are mostly vacant. Few

inhabitants are cautiously returning one by one to what was once their home. We are in the Luwero Triangle where thousands were ruthlessly killed by the military of previous regimes. Stacks of bleached human bones and skulls decorate the road-side near several villages. A grim reminder of the many civilians who perished in the civil war that has plagued this land since 1980. Thousands suffered so cruelly as their smashed skulls testify. They had cried out but no one answered, they had wept but no one heard.

At Masindi, we pause to fill the vehicle with diesel. While re-fueling we learn that there is heavy fighting at Kigumba. The fleeing U.N.L.A. soldiers have re-assembled themselves and are putting up stiff resistance. The N.R.A. are finding it difficult to dislodge them. We have come this far, do we turn back now? Our destination is but twenty-five miles away.

I decide to carry on. The army officer I spoke to at the hotel where he abides, advised me to take it one road-block at a time. They will be able to inform us of the latest development. So here we are bumping along the gravel road to Kigumba, the last leg of our journey.

At each road-block we find boys dressed in military fatigues. They are over-joyed at seeing us. To our enquiry as to how it is ahead their reply is always the same, "Maradadi tu!" ("Just lovely!") We reach a cluster of shops named after the mile post with the number Twenty-One. Here we turn off right and take a trail which will take us to Kinyonga just a few miles off into the bush.

Pulling into the station we surprise everyone. Ephraim thought because of the war we would not come. It has been bad here, he tells us. Many troops are parked at Kigumba. Stragglers of the previous regime are still in the nearby bush pushing their way north. Several gunshots are heard as we visit beside Ephraim's hut. His wife is with him. As soon as we are able we will be moving them back to Kampala where his office as the Executive Secretary Treasurer demands his presence more than here in the bush.

We are spending the night in the vehicle. Marion has a dreadful headache and is unable to sleep. The trip must have been too strenuous for her. I hold her close and ask the Lord to deliver her. Finally she is asleep. Was it wise to bring her along? Had I known that it is this dangerous, I would have insisted she remain at home. But then it gets tiring for her to stay behind. "Lord, be with us and the Christians this weekend. Amen."

We wake up to the squawking of francolins, a bird resembling the prairie chicken. I enjoy the mornings here at Kinyonga. Just enough bush around to house various birds. We will be holding classes throughout the day as scheduled.

About half of the enrolled T.E.E. students turn up in spite of the fighting. Mid morning the big guns go into action. They are at Kigumba, only four miles away when using the foot-path. One missile lands in the ravine less than three hundred yards from the church! The tin roof rattles and the singing inside misses several notes. Marion is just in her music class and I am correcting the test papers while sitting under a tree.

There is much shooting late in the afternoon. It comes from the direction of Mile Twenty One. Word comes that the old army is holding its own at Kigumba, and even repelling the N.R.A. at various positions. Many troops have been captured by the U.N.L.A. Both sides have suffered heavy losses in lives thus far. Civilians have also been killed as well as homes looted and burned.

Tonight many escaping from the nearby fighting are

bedding down on the station compound. They have accounts of horror to relate. Members in their families have either been beaten, tortured, raped, burned, kidnapped or killed. After words of comfort, I commit them into God's hands for safety throughout the night.

It is quiet this morning. Reports come in early. One has it that the U.N.L.A. has captured Kigumba and that the N.R.A. has retreated to Mile Twenty One. Another report says that Jeja is vacated. All the occupants have fled. That is the reason no one came from there to the seminar yesterday!

Sent Ephraim with one of the men from here by bicycle to Mile Twenty One for the latest news. The locals here want us to clear out before we are cut off. They are anxious for our lives. When the two do not show up at ten o'clock, we begin our Sunday service. My message is based on John 14:27, "I do not give to you peace as the world gives."

While the service is still in session, Ephraim and Jonathan walk in and share their news. They found no one along the route to Mile Twenty One. The trading center itself was deserted as well. The soldiers manning the road-block have retreated to Kizibu, the next village. The two then followed them there to converse with the commander who quickly informed Ephraim that the missionary is to leave immediately. The U.N.L.A. will be after his vehicle as soon as it is discovered. The news was not encouraging.

The meeting is closed with prayer where God is again beseeched to set a hedge about His children. Then we load our vehicle for our return to Kampala. Our plan to stay until tomorrow and then drive on to Alur in West Nile is now scrapped due to the continuing warfare which has cut us off from going any further. Ephraim's wife, Jova is to accompany us while he stays on to be with the Christians during this time of apprehension and uncertainty. They plan to retreat into the bush as soon as we leave the station.

At one o'clock we are ready to leave. We cannot go out the way we came. That route is now cut off. We have got to drive through the bush a distance and turn back to the road at Kizibu. Annah, who came with us from Kampala, now guides us to a cow-path which will take us there. She hails from here and knows all the bush tracks. The trail is stoney in spots and once the vehicle almost hangs up on one rock. The detour takes us through shrubby terrain. We are well hid from the main road.

When we are level with Kizibu, I swing the vehicle onto a path which leads us to the trading center. The residents stare at us. So do the soldiers at the road-block. After a few words of greetings we are on our way. It will be dark by the time we reach Kampala. We are thankful to the Lord for bringing us out of the bush safely in spite of our route getting cut-off. Throughout the whole ordeal of being caught amid the wars of the past six months, we never had any doubt as to His protection. Did He not promise that He will never leave us nor forsake us? (Hebrews 13:5). I am His apostle, a soldier of the cross. The words which Isaac Watts penned to a song come to mind:

> Am I a soldier of the cross,
>   A follower of the Lamb?
> And shall I fear to own His cause,
>   Or blush to speak His name?

Must I be carried to the skies
    On flowery beds of ease
While others fought to win the prize,
    And sailed through bloody seas?

Sure I must fight, if I would reign,
    Increase my courage, Lord.
I will bear the toil, endure the  pain,
    Supported by thy Word. Amen.

# Chapter Twelve
# Two Disciples

Rufus Akhonya, an Mluyia, is my age. I first met him
in Kenya back in 1974. He was the evangelist in Masai-
land where he had planted two churches. In the two
following years he and I added eight more. I found him
to be a man after my own heart, and the only one who
was willing to walk with me, the paths over the rolling
hills in search of Masai converts. He did not fear them,
as so many do. And they accepted him into their midst, a
feat not many accomplished when not their tribesman.

He often would share his dreams to reach out to other
tribes, and his desire to return to Uganda where he had
been during 1969 to 1971. None of us knew at the time
that his dream would come true and that God would also
put the burden on the heart of the listener that day in
1976 while we were traipsing from boma to boma in
Masai-land.

Before coming to Uganda, I received a letter from
Rufus stating he had heard we were returning to Africa.
Could he join us in Uganda to assist with spreading the

gospel? It takes only a few weeks after our arrival and we are re-united in God's work. The years of separation has not dimmed his zeal, only slowed his footsteps some. He has more lines on his face, more corns on his feet, and an asthmatic cough which wretches his frail body at times. At nights we will hear it after one of his up-country trips. If anyone deserves healing, he does. We have approached the Lord often about it. Instead of removing it, the Lord gives him more grace and endurance. Marion's good home cooking has done much to improve his health.

A more dedicated man in planting churches is difficult to find. He is obsessed with a desire to see congregations planted throughout the country. In this mountainous task that God has called me to perform in Uganda, He has provided the right man to assist me. Rufus has all the right qualities. He has proven to be a terrific example to the Ugandan church leaders as a consecrated and dedicated man of God.

When on safari up-country he travels with the minimum. Eats what the villagers set before him, and goes without when there is none. Sleeps where they put him, and stretches out on the floor in the bus park or police station should the night catch him in between points. Churches have grown in number rapidly not because of an abundance of financial assistance from abroad. No, it has grown because of the sacrifices of men!

Rufus is a man of prayer. When he arrives at a home he prays before seating himself. Upon leaving he again prays. Before and after meals he prays if given the opportunity. During seminars you will find him alone somewhere praying. Whenever he spends the night with us we hear him praying earnestly in his room before sleeping. One night I was awakened to the sound of him in the next room weeping and praying brokenly for his wife. Earlier we had given him a telegram which had arrived a week ago which contained the words—"Your wife is very sick, come home immediately!"

We part at Busia after making plans to meet again in two weeks time for our next seminar in the West Nile. He is to stop off in Lango and take Wilson Owiny our district chairman along to help him with visitation work until the seminar. We both did not know that day as we parted that unknown events would take place to foil our plans and to make it impossible to meet again for more than two months!

Arriving at Ojul in Lango where Wilson lives, they prepare themselves for tomorrow's safari to Agarokato where they will catch the train which will take them eventually to West Nile. Before retiring they sing with those who have gathered in the home. Then pray for their journey and ask God to watch over Wilson's wife who is expecting her fourth child.

Their ten-mile foot safari to Agarokato is without incident. Karamojong cattle raiders have been disturbing this area recently and locals are moving their livestock further away up-country. In the evening Christians gather at the church and God blesses their service. A child is dedicated to the Lord. They submit themselves into His care for the night and all is quiet.

Early in the morning many of them escort Rufus and Wilson to the station. They will not be forgotten in their prayers the two disciples are told as they board the train. At Gulu they must wait for the one from Pakwach. This means spending the night in the station eating a meager meal.

At midnight Wilson dreams that General Tito Okello, the head of state, is chased out of Uganda and flees to

Kenya. Upon awakening in the morning, he shares his dream with Rufus. If this were to come true there could be much trouble ahead! Rufus calmly says, "Let's place everything to God, but, I am sure your dream might come true. Sometimes it will take two days, or three without any change." Then they have a round of prayer.

They board the train and at noon disembark at Pakwach. Here a bridge spans across the Nile. The river is quite wide at this point as the water from Lake Victoria has now been joined by that from Lake Albert. The mighty Nile flows all the way through Africa from the equator to the Mediterranean Sea.

Here on the bridge the two are lightly checked at a military road-block. The sun is beating down on them as they climb up into the back of a lorry heading west to Nebbi. At the trading center Nyaravur, they drop off and rest for thirty minutes in the shade of a shop before attempting the last leg of their journey. Their destination is now only four miles to the south on a road which eventually takes one to Zaire. They walk it by foot and arrive in Pamora village where they are welcomed and shown love.

Their work now for the next nine days will be to visit and strengthen the out-lying churches here in Alur. This will include teaching, listening to their problems, praying for dedicated children and baptizing new believers.

On the second day of their itinerary they receive the news that Kampala has fallen to the guerrillas and the government of Tito Okello over-thrown. What about the missionaries? Will they still be coming to West Nile? Maybe it is not so bad. So with faith they push on determined to complete their mission. Villagers begin to worry but the two disciples for Christ keep encouraged.

Then, even in this remote area, they hear shooting!

Soldiers of the defeated army are starting to reach their homeland. Civilians are running and hiding, our two brothers joining them. One night they discuss how things have become worse. "Shall we continue staying here?" asks Wilson, "Until when?"

They know now the missionary is unable to come due to the closure of roads. They talk of crossing into Zaire but only one of them, Rufus, has a passport. Also, their money is slowly getting finished. To continue staying any longer will cut into their fare money as they are helping with food wherever they lodge. The two arrive at a decision. They will leave at once with the little that remains and use it for food on the way. To make it stretch they will walk. If they wait any longer they may not get out. The Spirit agrees at once with their decision.

After awakening the two inform the Christians of their plans to return to Lango. They are alarmed and beg Rufus and Wilson not to go. "You will be killed on the way!" they say. "The soldiers are behaving badly." But Rufus asks for someone to indicate the path which will take them on a short route to Alwii church. One of the men then volunteers to direct them to the place. It is a thirteen-mile walk and they arrive before night-fall.

When they reach the church leader's home they discover he is not there. They are now lost strangers. Fortunately, the two soon meet a boy who recognizes Rufus from his previous visits. He welcomes them to his brother's home as he is afraid of his father. The boy dashes away to fetch his brother but cannot locate him. It is getting dark so they try on their own to find a place for the night. Rufus enquires at a hut which is close by and she refuses them because the man is not present. They turn away, both disgusted by now and return to the place where they had been left alone by the boy. It is now dark and many soldiers carrying guns are passing on the road which comes from Pakwach.

But the Lord has not forsaken them. After fifteen minutes the boy appears with his brother who welcomes the two inside. They offer up a prayer of thanks. Then the man of the house fetches in some of the Christians living nearby and together they praise the Lord. The following day is spent encouraging the believers. When evening comes plans are made to push on at daybreak. At Pakwach they will know which direction to take. For Kigumba where Rufus has a home nearby, or for Gulu if the train is running. Or, for Lira and on to Wilson's home.

The two start off early. They have to make the thirteen remaining miles to Pakwach by noon if they are to catch the train. People had told them yesterday that it was still moving eastwards. In their bag is roasted cassava and the remainder of the sesame butter which Wilson's wife had sent along when they started their journey. Arriving in town they find no train and no vehicle moving eastwards! There are thousands of soldiers about behaving unruly. No one in control of them. The two disciples pray, "God it is your time now to care for us!"

Being hungry they take tea. "What to do next?" says Rufus. It is decided to cross over the Nile. "Let's buy some more cassava," says Wilson "to push us ahead." Frightened as they are, they approach the bridge. And God is with them. They find the soldiers are busily killing game in the park on the other side and ordering civilians to help carry the meat back into town. The two join those who are going and move hurriedly to the other side lest the soldiers change their minds. No one wants to be thrown over into the waters below.

They are now in the park with the bridge behind

them. For twelve miles they see no one, not even a lorry. Only the Uganda kob and spent shells along the way. There is no water to drink and they are tired. They push on. Then they stumble upon a stream. Here Wilson says to Rufus, "I'm going to drink this water." The reply is "Okay, but me I'm just washing my feet." Having done this the two set off again.

At a deserted road works camp they sit and rest for thirty minutes. Rufus now feels the pangs of thirst. Wilson tells him "When we were at school and wanted to drink water, and there was none we would eat green mangoes raw." He says this because mango trees are present in the camp. Rufus eats a few and feels a little better. They also consume some of their cassava before resuming their flight to safety.

Four miles later Rufus, who is already exhausted, gets very thirsty. Luckily enough it showers just then! A blessing from God. They push on for a short distance and Rufus says, "Wison, I am finished. Better we rest." The reply is, "But I tell you brother, we are within the park where there are no homes to beg for water!" Rufus sits down but Wilson refuses, sensing if he does he too will feel too tired to go further. Standing there looking down at his older companion, he recognizes the hoof prints of a buffalo at his feet. Frightened, he orders Rufus to vacate the area with him.

Rufus musters up courage and walks on even though he has long exhausted his store of endurance. A few steps ahead he sees a puddle of water which has collected on the center of the road. He requests a cup from Wilson so as to scoop up some of it to quench his thirst. "Are you going to drink this water?" exclaims his companion. "Just give me the cup." Taking it he drinks some of the muddy liquid. Will he now fall sick? "We best reduce our speed until we find a place to rest," Wilson tells Rufus.

They spot a grass hut at the park boundry. The two head for it and reaching it ask for help. His name is Daniel and he invites them to be seated inside. Water to drink and for bathing is given them and then food to eat. Before setting off the next morning they pray for the family who has shown them such good hospitality.

They trudge all day and arrive at a village called Purongo where the two spend the night in an old woman's home. They resume their foot safari the following day, covering over twenty-four miles. Wilson pushes Rufus on even when the latter wishes to halt for the night. It is in an area where strangers that stop over, disappear! Reports are that they are killed and eaten! And Wilson is aware of this.

At Gomba they have problems. They are now finished and want only to rest. But the home they go to does not welcome them. Instead, the occupants resent their presence so they get up and leave. Villagers are suspicious of any passing strangers now. Who is for what side? They are in Acholi country, the home of the defeated army. The two meet many soldiers, some harsh with them while others kind.

The next day they reach a village called Minakulo where Wilson looks up his brother David. The two are welcomed warmly and shown good hospitality in his home. The war is spilling northwards and their route to Kigumba is cut off! A heavy battle is raging at Karuma Falls to the south so the two are unable to go that direction to Kampala. Further more, fleeing troops are coming up from the east via Mbale and Soroti. To travel to Lira right now will also be unsafe! They may as well stay where they are and await further developments.

For a whole week it is peaceful at Minakulo. Then it

changes. Soldiers passing through shoot a villager and he dies. This frightens the rest of them and they run into the bush to hide. Near David's house one more is killed by the fleeing soldiers. This shocks the two disciples! The occupants of the home where they are staying gather up all they possess and conceal them in the bush. Rufus and Wilson are ordered to vacate and sleep outdoors with them. For the following week the bush is their sleeping lodge.

Food becomes scarce. Running day and night from place to place, they lose weight. Besides hunger, the two also suffer from the cold when it rains. Their blankets become coated with mud. The area has become very unsafe. But God sees them through and protects His two disciples.

News comes that Lira has been captured by the guerrillas who now are in charge of the central government at Kampala. This means that the looting army of the previous regime is now being pushed northwards. They could try to pass through the country side and reach Wilson's place at Ojul beyond Lira! This the two decide to do. The situation here is still insecure and it has been maddening being vagabonds. Only God has kept them sane and safe from the pillaging soldiers.

After spending twenty days in the Minakulo vacinity, Rufus and Wilson find themselves once more on the road heading eastwards. On the way they arrive at the river Tochi and discover it quite deep. They remove their clothing and wade through it holding their belongings up over their heads. Reaching the other bank the two dress and keep moving. Five miles down the road, Rufus notices his watch is not in his pocket. Then he recalls something dropping into the water while crossing the river! It was his watch. Nothing to do but push on. They enter the village Achaba where the two beg for a place to lodge for the night. A home invites them in and both eat well.

In the morning they continue their journey and spend the next two nights in villages along the route they take. Then the two disicples skirt the town of Lira, walking thirty miles so as to reach Bar where Wilson has his mother-in-law. Here they are well treated and given much food to eat. She also nurses their now blistered feet. The compassionate woman washes Rufus' feet who is very weary, thin and weak. The soles of Wilson's are raw as well, with most of the skin gone. Here now they rest.

When Wilson feels strong enough to travel, he wishes to complete their journey. He is anxious to see his family and home. But Rufus is unable. He needs more time. "Leave me here and come another day to collect me," he tells Wilson. So his younger companion strikes out alone. He is too near home to tarry any longer. Only twenty-two more miles left to foot through the bush! He stops at one of our chuches long enough to inform the pastor of Rufus back at Bar. He is to go with his bike and collect him.

Arriving home Wilson finds his people crying for him and Rufus, believing they are dead. Upon seeing him alive they begin praising the Lord. They too had met with hardships during his absence. The fleeing soldiers had looted, raped, killed, even burned their grain. Many Acholi soldiers had joined forces with the Karamojong cattle raiders and stolen livestock as far west as Ojul. Even Agarokato, the village where they had started their safari six weeks ago had been raided and pillaged. In fact, they struck the very day they had departed by train!

When Rufus arrives on the back of Peter's bike, the Christians come together and offer up thanks to God for what he had accomplished through different people in assisting His servants to return unharmed. These two disciples who had been counted as dead are alive and in their midst. It is now a time of recalling and sharing about their one hundred and eighty-five mile foot safari through the Uganda bush!

A week later we in Kampala, after two months of silence, see Rufus walk into our home. The days of waiting and praying for his and Wilson's welfare have ended. Thank you Lord for your mighty hand which reaches to the farthest corner! I send him home for a well deserved rest. But instead of staying the whole month given, he is back in half the time. "Where to is our next safari?" he asks.

# Chapter Thirteen
# Signs Will Accompany
# Those Who Believe

Several experiences among the Teso in Bukedi district revealed that many still cling to their traditional beliefs of animism. After the close of our service at a village where we were taken to open a church, one of the converts asks us to come to his home. He leads us to a hut wherein he keeps his paraphernalia which he uses in witchcraft. There is a leopard skin and a gourd containing bits and pieces resembling charms. There are four openings to this one-roomed grass roofed hut which he now asks me to burn down to the ground. He is giving it all up for Christ.

I tell him that he must do this himself. To receive complete victory over his old practice of being a witchdoctor he must light the match and set fire to the hut with its contents personally. He must go all the way for Christ. Will he? He does. We watch as the fire envelopes the building, burning everything inside. Then this young Christian asks for prayer so that Satan will not be able to draw him back into his old profesion again. This we do, asking the Lord to set a hedge about him and his house.

*     *     *

Returning to Bukedi district several months later to hold a seminar at Boliso, we find the father of George Muzei deathly sick. Talking to him before prayer he reveals that there is a tree which he dedicated to the evil spirits years before in the corner of his "shamba" (field). He recognizes that before God will hear his request the tree will have to be cut down. It was standing in the way of his healing.

The tree, a tall candelabra, is in a grove which has grown up around it, for it was planted years ago to appease the evil spirits. The old man, much younger then, had done this so that the demons would have a dwelling place and therefore leave him alone. Neighbours know of the tree and avoid passing too near the grove for fear of disturbing the demons.

All are quiet and sober as Marion and I file with the T.E.E. students through the banana plantation. Who will be the one to lay the axe to that tree? When we reach the spot, George, the old man's son, grabs the axe and swinging it back he shouts, "In the name of Jesus we come against you Satan!" The axe slices into the tree. Again and again. Chips begin to fly. Someone relieves George. The tree is hard and it is taking time for it to fall. Other young pastors take their turn at the axe.

Finally the tree begins to quiver. Ever so slowly it leans to one side. Then with an abnormally loud crack it breaks off and crashes to the ground. Marion leads them in a chorus, "Shetani ameshindwa" ("Satan has been defeated"). There is rejoicing amid the singing. The young men continue to wield the axe and chop down the surrounding trees until the grove is completely cleared away. Where minutes before we had been standing in total darkness, we now find ourselves bathing in bright sunlight.

Arriving back on the compound, we discover the old man dressed and waiting for our return. He informs us that when he heard the loud crack of the tree breaking off he felt a release in his soul and a voice telling him to get up! So he obeyed. Praise the Lord! God honored his sacrifice and healed him of his ailment.

*     *     *

It does not take long and George with his young pastors in Bukedi are busily praying for deliverance of those who are possessed by evil spirits. At one home to where they are called, they find a very sick man who is not responding to the medicines he has purchased. In questioning him they discover he has various charms. He is asked to cast them away. They sense there is something else. No use praying for him until the man's faith is in Jesus Christ alone. The patient finally confesses there is one more thing he is hiding.

Not far away on a rise there is a protruding rock, and under it lives a huge snake. He has been there for as long as the villagers can remember. Gifts of food are taken to him by those who believe in him, for surely he has power to bring evil if he is not appeased! The patient is one of those who is involved in this snake worship. He now wishes to break with it.

George and his colleagues march off to the hill which houses the old snake. Along the way the villagers attempt to discourage them in their quest to challenge the snake. The young servants of God are told they will die if they approach the snake too closely. But they

143

might as well save their breath for their advice falls on deaf ears.

They halt before the large rock. Then they spot the snake. He is lying at the base in front of an entrance which must be his lair. The snake is huge, and then they notice he has two horns like a serpent! The pastors approach nearer, binding him in the Name of Jesus. The serpent disappears inside. They gather brush and set it alight in front of the entrance to his lair. Smoke curls into the opening. As the flames increase in size, they notice, to their amazement the boulder begins to weep. Drops of water trickle down the face of the rock!

They wait until the fire dies down. And then it is out. During the whole episode the serpent does not make an appearance. In fact, it has never been seen again. The villagers have been set free from his satanic power. The patient who was ill recovers completely.

*     *     *

In Bunyoro district there is a concentration of inhabitants hailing from various parts of Uganda, including Kenya, Zaire and Sudan. Especially in the vacinity of Kigumba you will meet representatives from over fifty different tribes! Even the Karamojong are there. At least one thousand have settled into two separate villages villages in the bush, one of them near Kinyonga. They fled the fighting in their district and wished to live a quieter life elsewhere so they moved here in this district. This gives us an opportunity to learn about them and share the gospel with them. My desire and aim is to take the Word of God someday to this fierce and most disliked tribe up in northeast Uganda.

On our first visit to Kanyonyi near Kinyonga, Marion and I find the villagers not hostile but friendly. We have come to hold a service. On the way to the tree where in its shade the meeting will take place, we are ushered into a hut which contains a woman who is very ill. Would we have any medicine to help her? Marion does have chloroquine and aspirins with her for malaria, but this is not what she needs.

The woman is lying on a cow skin, her eyes closed and barely breathing. Instead of a fever she is ice cold. Then Marion discovers the patient has lock-jaw when she tries to force an aspirin into her mouth. There is just one thing left that we can do. And that is to pray. Marion and I lay our hands on the cold frail form and call upon the Lord to have mercy and heal her.

Her eyes begin to flutter and she attempts to say a few words. Marion leads a chorus of praise, "Asante sana, Yesu" ("Thank you, thank you, Jesus"). God is performing a miracle! The once locked mouth is now whispering words in her language. She is so weak and is unable to raise from her pallet. I tell her to rest as we are carrying on to the place of worship scheduled at this time.

It is a good service with many in attendance. They appear from every direction. Rufus had been moving about alerting them of our arrival. After praying for those who came seeking salvation, we stop in and see how our patient is faring. She is sleeping peacefully and under my touch I now feel warmth in her body. All she now needs is rest and food. With a word of thanks to the Healer we depart.

The following day a man from her village passing through Kinyonga informs us that she is right now digging in her garden. All her neighbours are rejoicing over her recovery. Truly a miracle! On our next safari to that area we recognize her at the service completely healed and happy in the Lord. Had we not gone that day with the Word, this woman may not be alive today to attend her family.

*       *       *

While in Busogo district, I drive deep into the bush to hold a service at a new church called Mawanga. Nearby there is a man dying, I am told. Would I stop in and pray for him on our way out after the service? And this we do. Walking into the hut, the woman points out her husband lying quite still on the floor wrapped in a blanket. He does not respond to our greetings. "How long has he been this way?" I ask his wife. "Not long. He just turned sick rather quickly and is steadily growing worse." Someone then says that witchcraft is suspected. It certainly has the full makings of it! No symptoms, just suddenly ill.

His wife is a Christian and I ask her to believe on his behalf as we pray the prayer of faith for his recovery. I simply ask the Lord to bring him back from death's door. In the name of Jesus I rebuke the powers of Satan. Before we leave the man comes alive and makes an effort to raise himself. We rejoice and praise the Lord for answering prayer. Rufus, Francis and I then leave.

Returning to Busoga two months later to perform a wedding at Mawanga, I notice the man we had prayed for earlier. He has fully recovered. Praise the Lord! I learn that before I had gone out of sight that day, he had gotten to his feet and walked about. A testimony of divine healing!

*       *       *

We are on a path which is taking us to a new church here in Teso district. The road we left miles behind us when we turned off to enter this bushy territory. Marion has often said, "It is amazing how we seem to plant churches in such isolated places! Why can we not be like others who have them situated along the good roads?" That is a good question. But Jesus did say to go into the by-ways as well, and not just the highways. He must have chosen us to go to the by-ways.

Twisting and turning to escape the thorny branches scratching our vehicle too much, we finally come to a halt at the village of Ogosoi where we will be spending the night. They have erected a small building in which they hold their services. After all the greetings are said we proceed to church and begin worshipping the Lord with our newly found brothers and sisters in the Lord.

One of those at the altar, after my message, is an old woman who is blind and crippled. I noticed her being escorted near to where I was standing while preaching. She has a long stick with her which she uses as a leaning post. After praying for those who have come with their needs, they stand up and return to their seats. Except the old woman who remains at the altar. I ask her what she is seeking. "I want to be healed," she answers. "Do you believe that Christ will do that for you?"

"Yes."

We lay our hands on her and pray for healing to flow through her body. I then feel the Spirit directing me to take her hand and command her to stand. She stands up! I then lead her outside and take away my hand. She keeps walking. Then I suddenly realize that she now can also see! The Lord has restored her sight as well. Thank you Lord! Here in the heart of Africa, in a remote village, Jesus has just performed a miracle of healing! An old lady can again walk and see.

*        *        *

Francis and myself are just coming from a ceremony where several boys in their teens were circumcised at Cheptui in North Bugisu. Previous to this we had witnessed much running and dancing on the road by the candidates and their escorts. All wore their customary dress for this occasion complete with colobus monkey skin hats and knobbed sticks. Their bodies were smeared in white and when they were circumcised not one of them uttered a word. When it was done, there was much dancing by the women and much drinking by the men who gathered around a huge pot and sipped the beer through long reeds which were at least six feet long.

On our way back to Makosia's home at Busia, the two passengers we picked up at Mbale accept Christ as their Savior. Francis witnesses to the one who drops off first, and then to the second one who is going as far as Tororo. He also makes dates to visit them in the near future in order to open churches at their villages. Any passenger who enters the Nissan is a candidate for salvation. Ephraim, Rufus and Francis have led souls to the Lord on many different occasions while I keep the vehicle rolling.

Arriving at his home after dark we discover that his twelve-year-old son has had an unusual day. Margaret, the wife of Francis, informs us that Martin awakened in the morning with a fever. She calls the pastor and his wife over to help pray for him. Someone else accompanies them who is immediately refused by the boy. Martin does not want him to lay his hands on him. Instead he commences to preach to him and to others who have congregated at Makosia's house. The text he uses is Matthew 3:2, "Repent, for the kingdom of heaven is near."

Afraid now to pray for him, they disperse. The boy lies

down to rest. A short time later, he gets up and exclaims to his mother excitedly that God wants him to go to a neighbour's hut, a mile away, and pray for the woman who lies ill with a wrenched back. The mother tries to reason with him that he himself is unfit to be up and around. But he heeds her not and runs off to do an errand that God has called him to perform.

He reaches her house on the run. Upon entering the woman feels healing flow through her body. She stands to her feet and finds that her pain is no longer there. God has healed her back! She accompanies Martin back to his home to testify to Margaret of her healing.

When his father has not returned by dark, he drops off to sleep. But before he does he gives his mother a portion of Scripture to give to his father when he returns. It is Luke 16:10-12. "Whoever can be trusted with very little can also be trusted with much, and whoever is dishonest with very little will also be dishonest with much. So if you have not been trustworthy in handling worldly wealth, who will trust you with true riches? And if you have not been trustworthy with someone else's property, who will give you property of your own?"

After Francis has read the Scripture his son has passed on to him from the Lord, he asks me, "What does this mean?" I answer him by saying that God wants him to be sensitive even in the small financial dealings. They are easily overlooked, but God wants us to give an account of even that. I add that apparently there is a reason for this warning. He should heed it and not let Satan deter him from being faithful, even in the small seemingly unimportant things.

The mother wishes me to pray for Martin so that he will be healed. I touch the sleeping boy's brow and detect no fever. Turning to her I say, "He is normal. He is not sick. The Lord just used him today to perform some duties for Him." And sure enough in the morning he is up and around. Before I leave he and his two sisters sing several songs for me.

# Chapter Fourteen
# The Little Foxes

Among Solomon's wise sayings there is one that has dogged me a lot. It is recorded in Song of Songs 3:15. "Catch for us the foxes, the little foxes that ruin the vineyards, our vineyards that are in bloom." We are most careful how we do the important things and try to keep from muddling up as much as possible. But where I have blown my best intentions and good deeds is when I was caught unawares in some minor incident which should never have happened but, unfortunately, did. It could easily have been done differently, I think. I will let you be the judge.

We pull into a remote area in Bugisu. Francis Makosia tells us we have started a new church here. The thing to do now is hold some special services this weekend where we will also show films on the life of Christ with the use of the generator we have brought along. We also intend to have various classes on Bible subjects, plus Marion teaching them new songs. We do this at all our districts so this one will be no different. Rufus is along, as well as our son Mark, who is with us from Canada for his summer holidays.

As the weekend progresses we run into a few snags. One of them is with the projector. It is not feeding the films properly. We work on it for over an hour one evening. It finally runs after some feverish praying. The hundreds of spectators who have been singing during the whole time breathe a sigh of relief when the picture comes on.

On Sunday a lay leader is chosen to lead the congregation. Part of his responsibilities will be to enroll in the T.E.E. program so as to learn his duties and to study the Word. The choice does not look like a prime example of a pastor, but then I have seen worse. There are a few hopefuls in the congregation that could take over should he fail in the process.

Monday morning arrives and we commence carrying all our things to the Nissan. I want everything at my feet before I pack them inside. I have learned, many backaches ago, that it saves on my energy by dong it this way. Yes, it is all here I am told. So in goes the generator. It is heavy and several spectators are needed to load it. Then comes the box of films, screen, the box of Bibles, the box of T.E.E. books, boxes of tracts, the box of cups and bowls, our sponge mattress and sleeping bag, Rufus's sponge mattress and blanket. Here comes more stuff. Rufus's bag, our suitcase, lunch box and water container, petrol can, a couple stocks of bananas and a chicken. I manage to tuck it all inside. The chicken I shove under the back seat.

We say goodbye to those standing around, shaking their hands and smiling sweetly. The weekend was a busy one and I am exhausted. Just loading the vehicle, making sure everything got inside made it more tiring.

Then, one asks me before I can step into the vehicle whether I can take along his son. What? Why didn't he say something sooner? "Where is he?" If he is only a lad I will squeeze him in I guess. Just then I hear chopping up in the banana grove above us. "He's just cutting two stocks of bananas to take along to school," the father replies. "He'll be here soon."

We are scheduled to be in another district some distance away this afternoon. No time to dilly-dally around. Don't they realize this? Besides how can I get two large stocks of bananas into an already full vehicle? To get the lad inside, who turns out to be at least fourteen years of age, is going to be a problem in itself. Why wasn't all this said before?

We have been here for three days. Even this morning before I loaded the car, it would have helped. It is the little foxes that ruin the vineyards. "No, I cannot take the bananas, there is no room." The boy then decides not to go as well.

Driving away, Marion says, "You could have maybe gotten them in somehow."

* * *

On the outskirts of Tororo, there is a road-block. We stop for it. After reading the church sign on the door, I am asked whether we can take along one policeman as far as Iganga which is a distance away. I ask, "There is only one person?" "Yes, only one," is the reply. They know church vehicles do not charge and so at road-blocks you are often stopped only to give someone a lift, either a policeman, soldier, or one of their friends. It can range from one to several in number, including their guns.

Reaching back to open the door for him to climb

153

inside, he steps aside and allows a woman to crawl in along with a child whom she is holding by the hand. Now wait a minute! Whose vehicle is this? I thought there is supposed to be only one passenger. What is happening here? Does he not know how to count? Out loud I say, "I was told there is only one passenger. Now who is the one?" They seat themselves inside, the man fetching along with him a tin of "posho" (maize meal) which he sets at his feet. Had not seen that before. My question goes unanswered.

This type of incident has occured over and over during the countless safaris thoughout Uganda. Very few are the occasions when it has a negative reaction on my part. This is one of those times. We just had a successful seminar in the east and are exhausted as we wend our way home. This makes it a lot easier for the little foxes to ruin the vineyard.

I do not order them out. No, I allow them to stay in the vehicle. There is space enough to sit beside Rufus and Wilson in back. They get their ride. But, they also get a lecture on dishonesty and why God cannot bless this country because of it. "I am a missionary you know and we have come to help, but we want people to treat us honestly. No country can prosper on corruption." On and on I went. I ended by giving them literature to read which we carry with us for the men at the road-blocks. They fell to reading it immediately, only too glad for the reprieve of my verbal discharge.

Oh yes, what I said was meaningful, right and fitting. But I am guessing that the Lord was not recording any of it. It just was not done in the proper spirit. The little foxes had gotten into the vineyard.

\*      \*      \*

I see the road-block ahead. We had passed through here three days ago on our way up to the West Nile. It is a lonely road but we had to take it in order to reach our churches in Alur. The usual route via Karuma Falls is presently unsafe due to rebel forces swarming through the park. Only lorries in a convoy under heavy military escort are permitted to traverse it. Even then a number of them had been ambushed at times. Our son, Kirk, was able to get his convoy of food from Kenya through to Sudan, for World Vision. It takes time though. Can run into weeks.

I pull my vehicle over to where the soldiers are loafing in the shade. It is a hot dusty day and the shade feels refreshing. Two of the six soldiers immediately snap at me, "Kwa nini ulipita road-block?" ("Why did you pass the road-block?"). Because of pulling my vehicle over into the shade I am now broad-side to their barrier which consists of a pole resting in the forks of two sticks. Technically I really have not passed it yet. But they see it otherwise. I explain that my coming into the shade has accommodated them. The two are still annoyed with me.

Many in the present army manning these out-posts are gradually resorting to tactics used by the previous army, looking for any flimsy excuse to acquire money from travellers. I do not offer them any. Instead, I say, "If I had wanted to pass your road-block, I would now be out of sight." In reality I would not have gotten too far before bullets from their automatic rifles would have splattered our vehicle and us inside. One barks, "Toa vyombo!" ("Take out your stuff!"). We all pile out and commence removing our belongings from the vehicle. He wishes to inspect our bags so we open them. The soldier had gotten his way. The gun made the difference.

No need to have a reason. No need to be merciful.

Miles later, as I pull onto the tarmac at Jeja, I hear a loud bang on the back of my vehicle. Slamming on the brakes, I ask, "Who did that?" A soldier appears and answers, "I did." "Why?" I was getting fed up by now of seeing camouflaged uniforms. The soldier goes on to say that he has a friend he wishes us to take along to Kampala. So that's how it is? The shoe is now on the other foot! Should I show them consideration?

The urge is to leave them behind. An eye for an eye! After all was I given any consideration back at the Biso road-block? They act as if the vehicle is theirs!

I could have saved my muttering for I end up taking him. There never was any doubt of that. What was it that I preached in the service yesterday? The text was I Peter 2:21-23, "That you should follow in His steps. He committed no sin, and no deceit was found in His mouth. When they hurled their insults at Him, He did not retaliate; when He suffered, He made no threats." Forgive me Lord. Help me to keep the little foxes out of the vineyard.

*     *     *

We were scheduled to be at Kamwenge in Toro district an hour ago—that is by my time. It certainly makes no difference to Elijah and Ephraim who are with me on this trip, as we wait for the villagers. After all they already had us for a service here last night! But I am not allowed to leave until we worship with them again.

I look at my watch again. Where are they anyway? Don't they know what time it is? Patience has always been one virtue that I have had problems with, even after all these years in Africa where you either have it or simply pack up. Oh, I have come a long ways, mind you.

I am still here in the land of "bado kidogo" (wait awhile).

The service did finally get started with nearly a hundred in attendance. Five accept Christ and three children are dedicated. As soon as I get everyone inside the vehicle, we leave amid a chorus of "Kwa heri" (goodbyes). Godfrey, our evangelist in western Uganda is present when we reach Kamwenge, but Rufus is no where to be seen. He is finally found two miles away at the railway station. Yes, he spent the night on the cold floor. Did not know where the site of the new church was so he just waited knowing that sooner or later someone will show up.

Sixty crowd into the room of the leader's house and ten accept Christ after my message. Give the one who will lead the flock his T.E.E. book. I believe a good start has been made here. Elijah takes time to teach the congregation until food is served at two o'clock. Meanwhile, Godfrey is informing me that many are waiting for me at Rwamwanja. "Where is Rwamwanja?" "It is only a few miles off the road on the way to Fort Portal." "Who told them I was coming?" "Did you not plan to drop in there?" 'No, that was not in the plan. My plan is to stay here and teach, then leave very early in the morning for Kampala via Fort Portal." Rufus confirms what I have just said. Godfrey is crest fallen.

After we have eaten, Ephraim says to me that it would not hurt to go and spend the night at Rwamwanja. "The people are really expecting us and will be quite disappointed," he adds. I can see Godfrey has been talking to him and has convinced Ephraim of the importance of the safari to Rwamwanja. There is a sign of rain and I pray, "Lord if you do not want me to go, let it rain before four o'clock." I need some confirmation of this sudden change in plans.

It does not rain. So here we are on our way to Rwamwanja. It is only twenty miles away, I am told by Godfrey. Should get there in good time for the service tonight. But the miles to an African is the same everywhere—longer when he must walk it, and shorter when he wants you to take him. I have a hunch it is so in this case. And it is.

I discover that we start counting the twenty miles only after we turn off the main track to Fort Portal onto a bush road! This means the twenty miles we have covered since Kanwenge does not count. Now I have with me six adults plus a sack and a half of maize for Elijah, two jerry cans of diesel, books and our travelling bags. In other words, we are loaded!

The road is very bad in spots, many big holes and wash-outs. While I am holding my breath and easing the Nissan gently through them, the six are lustily singing, "Tembea na Yesu, mpaka Rwamwanja" ("Walking with Jesus, until Rwamwanja"). They are oblivious to what the trip is doing to the vehicle. There is not one of them that believes we will not make it. And, maybe because of this the vehicle does transport us in one piece to our destination—Rwamwanja.

I am exhausted but the welcome is over-whelming. There are about one hundred seated under a shelter they have erected for the service. How long they have waited, I do not know. It is so common here to announce the arrival of the guest at a certain hour while knowing full well that it will never be possible for him to keep that appointment. So if I am delayed even more due to bad roads or vehicle trouble, then there is a very tired crowd. But how quickly they can bounce back to life is amazing.

The children cheer and clap. They sing for me. When they notice the blackboard, chalk and text books I have brought with me from Colleen, they are over-joyed. They sing some more for me. As the last rays of light fade, I close my message, but not the service. For after I have prayed for the ten who have received salvation, there are introductions and speeches with more singing.

While waiting for our meal in the leader's home, Elijah leads three more to the Lord. He is enjoying himself immensely on this safari with us! The week away from his pastorate in Kampala is a refreshing change for him. It is eleven o'clock before I retire to my Nissan. But, before I can climb in, the maize, diesel and books have to be removed. Willing hands are there to do it for me. No one is ready for bed. Only me.

Before I drop off to sleep, I cannot help but think, "What if I had allowed the little foxes to enter the vineyard back at Kamwenge? All this would not have taken place here at Rwanwanja. No rejoicing, no souls saved, no fellowship. "Thank you Lord for assisting me in mending the fences."

*　　　*　　　*

The lorry is ready to leave Kinyonga for Kampala. Some of the maize we have come for is loaded and so is the choir. Dedication of the Day Care Center at Kasubi takes place tomorrow so we need to hurry back. Stopping at Kigumba for more maize before commencing the hundred kilometer trek. I check the choir that is in back of the Benz to make sure that they have not exceeded the number allotted. At least twenty-eight wanted to come but it was shaved down to eighteen. There just is not sufficient room to accommodate more in the city.

My count reveals the number exceeds eighteen. But I am informed that many will get off at Kigumba when we stop for the maize. Turning around I notice Paulo's daughter standing nearby. She is one of those dropped from the twenty-eight. Approaching me timidly, she asks, "May I go along?" She is dressed in a dirty gown. I quickly answer, "You are not ready to go, you have no clean clothes for tomorrow." I thought this was a more polite answer than a straight, "No." Then she shows me her tiny bundle which I had not noticed earlier. "Here are my clothes," she says.

There is something tied inside a piece of cloth the size of my handerchief. She has no more. I turn quickly away before she can notice the tears that are beginning to fill my eyes. How can I refuse this girl? She has no right to go. What do I do? I turn to face her and motion for her to climb aboard.

At Kigumba those not going on to Kampala drop down. I count those remaining and come up with one too many. Peering at their faces, I discover a girl who was not in the group selected to go on to Kampala. I ask her to step forward and climb off the lorry. She stands up from where she is hiding behind one of the other girls. Quietly she approaches me. When she halts I ask her to descend. She does not. Only looks at me with pleading eyes which are saying, "Please, let me go along."

I look around for help. Ask the choir leader whether she is to stay behind. He answers that she is not one of those chosen to go. I was hoping he would take over now and talk her into staying home. He tries, but she ignores his commands to descend. Then I notice something on her right cheek-bone. It is a tear. It clings there a moment longer and then slowly caresses down her dusty cheek leaving behind a wet streak. Her left eye is full to the brim but she is able to keep that tear from falling. She has won the contest without having to say a word.

The following day as I sit listening to the choir at the dedication service, I spot the two girls who nearly missed being here. In the second one's eyes there is now a sparkle instead of tears. Had I allowed the little foxes to enter the vineyard, these two girls would have remained behind in the bush, never to see Kampala. And, miss singing for our guest from Germany, Reinhard Berle. Thank you Lord for helping me to make their dreams come true.

# Chapter Fifteen
# Hard Pressed But Not Crushed

Travelling to North Bugisu, our first stop on a twelve-day safari which will take us to five districts, we pass through numerous road-blocks. At the Busia turn-off, I find Rufus and Francis Makosia waiting. They will be assisting Ephraim and me at the seminars.

It is not long and Rufus shares his latest dream. We have learned to perk our ears when he relates those he deems repeating. He has told us that any dream he has after midnight comes to pass. This is one of those. He had one similar just before the coup. Are we going to under-go another change of government? In his dream he saw us running from a troubled area! It is fortunate that I persuaded Marion to remain at home. She had wanted to accompany me but I felt it may be dangerous up in Lango district where there have been repeated attacks by rebels recently.

Before arriving at Bunangaka, we pause to greet the Christians at Mpogo. We discover most of them missing. An old man who has remained shares how the Karamojong raiders appeared several days ago and ran off their cattle leaving behind several owners dead. He adds that Bunangaka, where we are heading, is still dangerous.

Reaching our destination, we are informed that raiders have struck in every direction. Many residents have moved away with their livestock. Most of the pastors are present though to greet us and to be in this weekend's seminar. In the evening service two receive Christ following the message delivered by Ephraim. When ten thirty arrives, we retire to our respective places. Mine is in the Nissan patrol. It is parked on James the district chairman's compound. I am ready for sleep.

An hour before midnight, dogs commence barking excitedly. The occupants of homes become alert. The owner of the home wherein Ephraim, Rufus and Francis are just bedding down for the night, informs them that Karamojong are around. The behaviour of the dogs has revealed that to him. He then advises them to vacate immediately, before the raiders strike. They grab their travelling bags, plus their sponge mats and set out into the night. Michael, the owner of the hut, leads the way to a grove of trees beside a running river. Rufus recognizes it as the one where we have held baptismal services.

In a heavy under-growth an opening is found and they crawl into it. There is room enough inside to spread out their mats on the damp ground. This will have to serve as a lodge for the night. Then, above the rushing water they hear a rifle being cocked! All stampede from their hiding spot, creepers and branches snatching at their clothing. The first one in becomes the last one out. Their bedding and bags forgotten behind.

Running low along the river bed, they become separated in the darkness. Suddenly someone looms up in front of David, one of the pastors. A Karamojong! He cries out. The man motions him to be quiet. "It is me, Francis," he whispers. Meanwhile, Ephraim and Michael have stopped running and lie down in some covering. It does not take long and they sense there is someone else nearby. They can hear his breathing. "Who are you?" they whisper. The reply which comes back is hoarse and unintelligible. Can it be Rufus? They are afraid to ask again lest they are heard by the enemy.

They all crouch in the grass and brush, tense and alert. Francis is with David, Ephraim with Michael, and Rufus on his own. No one dares fall asleep. They pray that God will protect the missionary who is sleeping in his vehicle not more than half a mile away. It is unsafe to make their way to him and warn him of the danger. They rely on God to be with him.

Just after midnight Ephraim and Michael creep back to where they had left their belongings. Here they remain awake until Francis, David and Rufus rejoin them in the approaching dawn at six o'clock. Tired, but now relaxed, they appear an hour later to relate the night's events. As for me, I slept the night through, unaware of the hardships my friends had endured. Only once had I been awakened, around one thirty, just to hear those who were spending the night with James still talking in a low tone. Breathing a prayer I succumbed to sleep again.

The three decide that we should not spend another night here. "The raiders will not fail to strike tonight!," I am warned. Last night turned out to be one of scouting and tonight they will not miss coming out in full force. Especially now that they know there is a vehicle present with a European who must have come with money. An opportunity such as this will not be passed. "Should you resist them, you will be killed," Ephraim adds. I realized then if I do not leave I will be placing them in danger as well.

In spite of the urgency to move on, I carry on with the seminar. All day there are classes with Ephraim, Rufus and I taking our turns in teaching. The district meeting is held as well. Then before the day closes we hold the service which was planned for next morning. I deliver the message the Lord has laid on my heart and then pray for those who seek His help. Committing the congregation and the pastors into His hands, we bid them farewell. It is now dark. We climb up the escarpment and stop near the Sebei border to spend the night at a vacated agricultural training school.

Luckily Marion stuck in several pieces of cooked liver and some roasted groundnuts. These I now share with my team mates in the morning. Then at a small shop at the Bugisu/Sebei border we order some tea to wash down the remnants of our breakfast. Peering out the little shop we are in, I spy drums of molasses stacked on the other side of the road. "It is used for brewing pombi," Francis says. I ask him to remind me on our way back to purchase a gallon of it for Marion. His eye brows raise, "Why?" "For cooking, of course," I reply.

In Sebei district the story is not much different. Karamojong have been raiding up here as well. Their cattle have been taken and their women raped. Here their story is that Bagisu are numbered among the rustlers. The Karamojong do not circumcise their young men, the Bagisu do. It makes sense that there should be informers.

Immediately after arrival Rufus assists the owner of the compound we will be staying on, to erect a shower. The reason is, of course, that the Mzungu must have a private place to bath. But, secretly my companions enjoy this luxury as well. Rufus has repeatedly said that when he travels alone he does not receive half the welcome as when he is with me. He seldom hears the squawking of a chicken as it runs for its life, but eventually to be caught by one of its chasers, usually a child, beheaded, plucked and cooked for the missionary with his companions who have just arrived.

Besides their language some Sebei customs resemble those of the Masai. One of them is to circumcise both their girls and boys as their sister tribe still does in Kenya and Tanzania. It is rainy here and the nights chilly. I forgot to put my rubber boots into the vehicle before leaving home. And this time I really am in need of them. The seminar and the services go well. We see souls saved each time one of us preaches. Francis gets his turn and has a fruitful response. We travel on the third day to a church near a beautiful waterfall and stay the night. The residents are glad to see the missionary. "We will be safe tonight," chirps a toothless granny. She believes with the man of God's presence among them the enemy will not strike. Has no one told her that we fled from Bunangaka? The night does pass peacefully. The folks here have been sleeping away from their homes for some time fearing the raiders' return.

Our next seminar is in Teso district. The drive down the escarpment from Sebei has a panaramic view of the plains below which stretches out as far as the eye can see. In the distance are the mountains in Karamoja jutting upwards, each one with their peculiar shapes. Not many of them and rather spread apart with miles and miles of nothing between them. Someday soon I plan to be in that vast lonely scene below for I wish to reach these fierce Karamojong with the gospel before my departure for furlough.

I drop off Francis in Mbale, he is to go on to South Bugisu where we will meet him on our way back from

Lango. Here we pick up Wilson as pre-arranged. He is on his safari back from Alur where we had left him two weeks earlier. He is to assist us along the way until we reach Lango where he lives. His new duties as the regional evangelist for the north has kept him busy and away from home a lot.

Only half of the pastors in Teso are present for the seminar. This district has been over-run with the raiders as well, not once or twice but many times. A band of them are camped just across the small lake from where we are standing here at Agule. Our church Gweri is on that side. We learn that a number of young men have gone into the bush to join the rebel forces after being accused and beaten countless times by the present army.

A large raiding party consisting of rebel forces and Karamojong cattle thieves swept through a week ago. No cows can be seen anywhere. They have either been stolen or moved to safer territory. We noticed as we were coming, men and women carrying items on their heads, or bikes, which they had scooped up before fleeing for their lives. They are on their way back home. When will all this stop? The government seems powerless to control the movements of the raiders who actually are spreading out more than ever, attacking villages which never had this problem before.

Our classes go well in spite of half the students not present. In the evening services souls are saved and others revived. They surely needed it. The nights spent in Teso are quiet. We had been told that there has been shooting nightly before our arrival. We are presently on the edge of territory where the rebels strike at will whenever and wherever they wish. Beyond Soroti you travel at your own risk. We have a seminar planned in Lango district and so we drive on to have it, Lord willing.

We reach Dokolo in Lango without a mishap. The road-block just outside Soroti does not have much to do as the traffic is almost non-existant. Turning off the main road which carries on to Lira, I take a bush road and move slowly between the trees to reach Acandyang the place of our seminar. Our arrival lifts their spirits! The churches in Lango have appreciated our appearances throughout the difficult times. I am thanked over and over for making the effort to keep our scheduled seminar.

The Lango have suffered much in the last two years. The coup saw the victorious army rumble through pillaging, looting and destroying everything in its path. Then the war saw the fleeing army repeat the same thing. Now they still are the recipients of mistreatment, once from this side and then from that side. They remain with nothing. Always on the run, the bush more their home than their hut. "Please Lord, bring peace to this broken land. Smite the enemy so that he cannot rise again! Amen."

The accounts the pastors and lay-leaders relate are heartbreaking. Each one of them has lost something or everything. Each one has had the experience of hiding in the bush or tall grass watching their possessions being taken or destroyed. Some relate how while hiding they could almost reach out and touch their enemy who was wearing very little besides the band tied tightly around his forehead and calves. They were gazing straight ahead, not turning their head to the left nor to the right but held in an upright position, pumping high their legs as they pounded by them.

As the raiders were approaching his house, the pastor broke through the wall in back and escaped with his family. Anyone who is spotted escaping is shot and often hit. Anyone caught is an object to be beaten or a candidate for rape. Two of our district leaders do not put in an appearance. Reports reaching us are that at the one place as he was preparing to come, raiders appeared. He was severely beaten and his properties stolen. At the other place there was an attack as well. The man escaped by running but his wife was captured and mis-used. All we are able to do to help them right now is pray, which we do.

As I turn in for the night, Christians who have come for the classes and services bed down on the compound in front of my vehicle. The first time for them not to sleep in the bush for three weeks! Will the enemy strike tonight? One who visited with us tonight on his way from Lira stated that cattle had been stolen two days ago near town. And reports have it that they are on their way in our direction! Our last seminar in Lango ended a success. But, alas, two days later thousands of rebels spilled down from the north, spread out miles wide, and swept through the very area we had just left! "You have kept watch over us thus far, Lord, continue to do so please. Amen."

Two weddings are performed. The grooms of both are pastors. No need for big ceremonies as both couples have been living together for years. They were married earlier in their traditional way under the dowry system. All that is required now is to promise before the Lord to keep their vows and to evoke His blessings on them. We expect all servants of God to fulfill this requirement as soon as possible. Then there is another couple who have just been re-united after living apart for years. Their marriage had been performed in a church. We pray for them and ask God to refresh their vows.

It is the season for flying ants. The Lango catch sacks full of them by attracting them to the light when it is dark. We are fed these insects twice daily prepared in three different ways—fried, cooked and roasted. The first dish, I have tasted on several occasions. But it is my first for the second and third dish. I end up eating the most from the dish of roasted ants which have been pounded into a paste resembling peanut butter. They give me two jars of it to take back for Marion and the rest. Raved too much, I guess, about how good it tasted. I'm anxious to see how they take to it?

In the district meeting I learn a church has been planted in Acholi district. Praise the Lord! An in-road has been made into rebel territory. Wilson will be going up there and with God's help open a few more. Before leaving Lango, I lock my key inside the vehicle accidently. This happens at Atur where we are holding our second service of the day. Managed to slip the stiff wire someone found for me over the closed window and hook the knob. It came up after a few tries.

We reach Bunyanga in South Bugisu before night-fall to a muddy welcome. Francis is waiting for us. It has rained heavily here today. The spot chosen for me to park my vehicle during our stay is in front of someone's house on the side of a hill. Water is gushing down in torrents as the Nissan bravely attempts to climb up the greasy knoll. But, alas, it has to be assisted by willing hands before it comes to rest caked in mud from one end to the other. It will be quite a feat to sleep in it tonight facing downwards as it is. There is nothing level here. It is either up, down or sideways.

We immediately slip and slide our way on foot to the shelter they have erected for the seminar. Really need my rubber boots now! At least three hundred are present and it being Palm Sunday, I preach on how Christ wept for the lost on that day long ago. Over one hundred crowd to the altar for prayer at the close of the service. They have come for salvation, healing and deliverance from demons. There seemed to be no end to people seeking God's help. The following day half as many are again at the altar when Ephraim finishes with his sermon.

I am discovering there is much demon possession here in this remote place. As soon as the anointing comes upon me, while praying for the sick especially, demons commence making a display. There is a trembling in the person which increases until he is thrown to the ground. At the same time he is either hissing like a serpent or grinding his teeth and muttering something unintelligible. One clubs me across the back of my neck and shoulder as I am praying for someone else. But one by one the possessed are delivered and set free from the demons. Many flee immediately upon hearing the name of Jesus, while others resist stubbornly and a battle commences for the soul of man. I hang onto the person to prevent him from falling face down in the mud as the demon wrestles with the power of Jesus' name. Finally the demon releases his captive and is gone. Praise the Lord!

There is much witchcraft practiced in the foothills of Mount Elgon. Could this be one of the reasons for such demon activity? Here, we are tucked back into a corner flanked by a mountainous range on two sides and inhabited hills on the other sides. What secrets lurk in this misty remote area? I am discovering a few slowly.

After our classes, Francis leads the candidates to the rushing river below and baptizes forty-nine in it. Here is where one roving "prophet" with his followers nearly drown a man in an attempt to dislodge the demon which they claimed he possessed. Just previous to this they had beaten him severely and failing to drive out the demon they drug him into the river. This same man who calls himself a prophet has appeared and asked to be accepted as one of our ministers. I tell him he is not fit to be called a servant of God. His actions are not becoming of a man with such a high calling. When asked to explain how we receive salvation he is unable to answer. He turns out to be a false prophet.

Before we are able to leave in the morning, after spending two days and nights here in the clouds, a woman appears asking for prayer. She wishes to be healed. We take time for her and then we are on our way. I have agreed to call in at two churches along the way for services. Of course, this includes a meal, I have learned that. Am told that they are located beside the road so I should make it back to Kampala before dark. I cannot help feeling that things may not be as they appear. Be prepared for the little foxes!

Leaving the vehicle in the shade of a tree not far from the road, we commence climbing up the side of a steep hill. The church is not near the road but up a mile, I am now politely informed. We clammer up the foot-path and leap across a stream which I do not clear properly. I end up with water in one shoe and mud splattered all the way up my trousers. How I miss my rubber boots! Yes, the hike is not one mile, but more like three. We arrive at Bumakuma church, my shirt soaked in sweat.

Twenty come for prayer after my message. A demon reacts in one, chattering and shaking the woman. Placing my hands on her I bind the spirit in His name. The demon leaves and she is at peace. We are fed a delicious meal before descending back to the vehicle. The hillside swarms with the Christians who are escorting us down. With amazing agility the youth skip along the steep path and leap across the stream with the ease of a gazelle. Of course, I did not have my camera ready. Unfortunately, the best photos I possess are in my mind only.

At the second church which I was told is situated right beside the road is actually a mile up the hill-side. Here at Bubulo we are introduced to a young man who turns out to be the one that was severely beaten and nearly drowned by the false prophet back at Bunyanga! We witness the scars across his shins, arms and on his head. His brother adds that blood and matter drained from his ears for some time. He now appears dull. Has his brain been affected? My heart is touched and I feel the impulse to pray for him. I want the Lord to heal him and restore him to normality. It is not right that some false prophet did this in the guise of being God's servant. This wrong must be made right.

After Ephraim's message, and the sixteen who have knelt for prayer are looked after, I call the young man to step forward. The Spirit's anointing is upon me as I lay hands and feel healing flow down into him. The witness is there that Jesus has healed him! Thank you, Lord. We then are served our third meal of the day before we are allowed to depart. It is difficult to say farewell to those who have escorted us back to the vehicle. But the sun does not tarry on its westward flight. We sing as we usually do while pulling away. And then we are down the road.

Driving on by Mayenze, Francis points out that in yester-years cannibals resided in this area. As a result no churches are to be found here to this day. The fear for this clan still exists. No one agrees to be invited to their homes for you may sit on a seat that is standing above a pit covered with a mat. After falling into it they commence clubbing you to death. You are then boiled and eaten.

Upon seeing a lone person, or stranger approaching,

scouts up in a tree begin passing the word along. They would say in their language "a grasshopper is coming." The doomed person does not suspect that he is the grasshopper for the residents in that area do catch and eat that insect. Someday, I know, we will have a church in this backward place where the pastor will accept the invitation to enter their homes—and they will be saved. "Lord, hear this prayer of mine."

We arrive safely back in Kampala just at dark. The safari we began twelve days ago with a warning which was fulfilled when we fled from North Bugisu, ends with putting Satan to flight in South Bugisu. As Paul so fittingly wrote—"We are pressed on every side, but not crushed." (2 Corinthians 4:8).

# Chapter Sixteen
# Contrary Winds

Marion is accompanying me on this safari which will take us to three districts in the east. We will be on the road nine days. Ephraim is with us and so is Margaret our house help who hails from Samia. A chance for her to see her mother. Arriving in Busoga we find Francis Makosia who will travel with us throughout as well. Rufus is not with us this time. He is stranded out west in Toro district due to the train not working.

Upon arrival we are notified that the site for our seminar has been shifted to another church deep inside. I know the route. The way is filled with deep holes. We are thrown from side to side as we traverse it. With us is David a pastor from North Bugisu. He shares of his flight from his home at Bunangaka when Karamojong raiders swept through only days after we had left for Sebei. From Siroko to Atari the Bagisu have vacated their land and are seeking refuge nearer to Mbale town.

"In the dark of the night they struck," says David. "My brother and I ran in one direction while the parents in another. It's everyone for himself from now on." The two manage to stay ahead of the fore-running raiders who are madly yelling and firing their weapons. The two keep running until they are tired. "Our end is near," thinks David. On a plowed field they drop flat on their stomachs, and watch the horde pound by them. "They were so close! My heart stood still."

Then they could hear cattle coming. The Karamojong had commenced driving the livestock, and the two were lying in their path! They dare not move. On came the beasts. Miraculously the cows avoid stepping on them! How they spotted them in time on the ground, in the dark is a miracle. The drivers with eyes only for their captured herd, sprint by the two. David then gets the urge to join them and soon both of them are sprinting along side the rustlers with no one paying attention to them. In the dark they pass as one of the Karamojong.

Entering the tree line the two slip away from them without being recognized. They are exhausted by now and lie there panting. Suddenly bullets commence flying in their direction. More Karamojong are coming covering the back trail of the captured herd. They are firing wildly into the bushes where David and his brother are hiding. Will one find them? The two force themselves to be still and not run. Then several halt not far from them and discuss something. Why don't they move on? Eventually they do.

David and his brother do not move from where they are until broad daylight. They see no one on their return trek. At home there is no one. The place is vacant. They manage to find three chickens which have been over-looked by the raiders. Soon the two are on their way down the road with the surviving hens. Several miles later one is sold, rather cheaply, and with the money they purchase a ticket to Mbale on the bus. The second one is sold, again cheaply, to carry them on to Tororo. Here the last hen assists them to complete their journey to their destination at Busia. They have sought refuge at the home of the only person they know who will help them—their regional chairman, Francis Makosia.

"What about James, our district chairman?," I ask David. He does not know. The day he and his brother left North Bugisu his house was empty. "He must have managed to take his family and himself out in time," David tells us. I guess we will know more when we pass through there on our way to Karamoja after this safari is over. Our prayers are with him and all those who have been driven from their homes. David adds that the Karamojong have given notice that they do not want any of them to return!

There are now twenty-four churches in Busoga district. This means I am busy throughout the seminar correcting their test papers when I am not teaching or in a meeting. Marion is treating the sick during her free time with medicines she has brought along for this purpose. There are ten candidates wishing to be baptized. Francis leads them out to the small river two miles away and baptizes them. By evening I discover I am being bothered by lice. At first I thought it was dust falling from the grass roof. But then we learn they are coming from the chairs we are using. Chickens stay in the house from where the chairs were brought. There is no outdoor enclosure for a shower, so a splash bath from a basin has to suffice. We are asked to go behind the house to take it. Fortunately for us the moon is a late riser tonight.

I am well pleased with the progress shown here under the leadership of their chairman Moses. We leave on schedule for Samia our next district. At the main road we look for diesel to fill our vehicle. There has been a fuel shortage for months now. I have never seen it like this since our arrival to Uganda. In Kampala, lineups three and four deep can be seen stretched out for blocks at filling stations which have received just enough to last a day or two.

Here at a bus stop near Bugiri, I show Marion where I came close to being shot by a trigger happy soldier several months ago. I was on my way to the church which we have just come from now. It was my first time to this new place so I am keeping my eyes glued to the turn-off which Francis keeps telling me is just ahead. "Control, control" he is saying. Then there is the loud report of a rifle! What happened? I look at Francis beside me, who has his head out the window and staring back. What he sees is revealed in his voice, "Stop and reverse! A soldier is shooting at us!"

No one had noticed the flimsy barrier. Busily talking and watching for the turn off, our attention was else where. The absence of any soldiers, who must have been in the shade somewhere, added to my easy passage of the road-block. The crack of the rifle brings me to a stop one hundred feet beyond it. What Francis now sees is the soldier dropping to the ground taking aim for a second shot. Failing to stop when I did, a bullet or two would certainly have ripped into our vehicle and someone hit.

Halting the Nissan beside them, there are four soldiers visible now, and the one who had fired his weapon is furious. Commands us to step out and remove what we have inside the vehicle. They discover that we carry only Bibles and T.E.E. books. Assuring them we are ministers of the gospel and not law breakers, they consent for us to proceed. Only a week later this same trigger happy soldier shoots and kills a young man on a bicycle who fails to stop at the barrier. This incident upsets the populace and they force them to move their road-block a mile from the village. The soldier was taken into custody.

One cannot be overly cautious at roadblocks. I recall vividly irate men in uniform swarming around us with itchy trigger fingers at another roadblock a year ago. Tim and Colleen had just picked us up at the airport where earlier Marion and I had flown in from Khartoum after spending a week with Kirk and Karen in Sudan. We have found this group of heavily armed soldiers on the outskirts of Entebbe rude and unmannerly. As we pull up to it we are on the end of a long queue. A hundred yards beyond this roadblock is the one for on-coming traffic.

Young men in fatigues crowd up to the vehicle when it comes our turn. One asks, "Mnatoka wapi?" ("Where are you coming from?") As if he doesn't know! Marion and I are in back with our luggage behind us. One soldier glances at it but does not demand to see it. Then the one who addressed Colleen and Tim waves us ahead. As the Nissan draws away I gaze back over my shoulder at the soldiers. One of them has his arm raised. Does he want us to stop? I mention it to Tim. Then there is a shout! Something is amiss!

A soldier runs towards us from the roadblock ahead of us. He is barking, "Leta silaha, leta silaha!" ("Bring the weapons, bring the weapons!") Tim skids to a halt and reverses to the head of the queue. We are quickly surrounded by men in uniform who order us out of the vehicle. Opening our suitcase I inform the officer in Swahili that we are missionaries and drove off because we were given permission by one of his men. It happens all too often that at roadblocks one soldier does not know what his comrade is doing.

The man with the gun fingers through our belongings. More curious than suspicious. Then as quickly as it started the whole affair ends. The officer has lost interest and orders us to proceed. We breathe a sigh of relief. Thank you Lord for delivering us from this tense and dangerous situation!

In Samia we have twenty churches. We are busy here as well. A wedding is squeezed into our full schedule. Ephraim performs it. The groom is one of our pastors. Marion meets with the women's group after her music class. In the evening service twenty six come for prayer after my message. Ten remain for the prayer of healing. A demon reveals itself in one and shakes her fiercely. Calmly placing my hand on her head, I command it to leave her in the name of Jesus! And it does. She is delivered from it's possession. Praise God! Two children are dedicated to the Lord before the service is dismissed.

Many insects resembling flying ants, only smaller, have invaded the hut we are in tonight. The lantern to which they are being attracted is moved back a distance so that we can eat our food undisturbed. Our vehicle is parked under a tree that was struck by lightning in the last rain storm a few days ago. Does lightning strike twice in the same place? I breathe a prayer that it will not as Marion and I crawl into the Nissan for the night. There is lightning on the horizon.

A woman with tuberculosis is brought to me soon after we have had our morning meal. She has had the disease for at least ten years, her relative tells me. Doctors have helped her very little. She loses very much blood coughing, as much as a bowl full at a time. "Do you have any "dawa" (medicine) for her?" implores the man. I tell him we have no medicine for her. The disease has wrenched her body so much that only the skeleton is remaining. Her days remaining here on earth are but few, unless. . . .

"There is One who is able to heal you of your disease," I tell the woman, "In fact, Jesus is the only One who can at this stage." I share with them how we can be healed of our diseases if we but believe in Him. When I feel her responding to the message, Ephraim and I lay on our hands and commence praying. In the Name of Jesus I command the disease to dry up and healing to return into her body. She begins to shake violently and to gag. There is something abnormal here!

It is a demon and is refusing to release her. I command it in the Name of Jesus to come out of her. The woman wrenches and there is a gurgling sound. I persist in calling on His name. Then, the demon vacates her. She suddenly is calm. An immediate transformation is taking place! Praise the Lord for His miraculous power. Where previously she was reclining on the grass, we see her now visiting with others before walking on home.

We reach Busiro mid morning in spite of one rear brake heating up on us. Could not find any serious problem inside when I opened it on the road. The district chairman for the Islands resides here and he will be escorting us to the churches in Lake Victoria. He tells us we will not leave until the winds are right for sailing, which may mean as late as midnight. Marion busies herself treating the sick which have come while I give out the tests to the T.E.E. students. In the evening service Ephraim preaches the message. I pray for the seventeen children who are brought for dedication.

Since we have time to spare on our hands tonight, the business meeting is held and the committee is appointed to assist the chairman in this new district. Mosquitoes are plentiful. I have found in all my travels only one other place where we have a church which exceeds Busiro with aggressive mosquitoes. And that is Kapiri in Teso district. Rufus and I were literally driven out of the hut we were eating in to complete our evening meal beside the fire outside. Even then I had to sit on the smokey side in order for them to leave me alone!

The wind is slow in switching direction. It is due to the rain that is threatening to come our way. Only a shower reaches us though. Then at one-thirty in the morning we are told all is ready. By the time we get down to the boat, just over a mile away, the wind should be in the right position to speed us on our way to Lolui Island. It is planned to visit our farthest church first and then work our way back. Lolui is sixty-five miles into Lake Victoria from Busiro. If the winds are right we should reach our destination in six hours, we are told.

Marion and I are taking along our sleeping bag and sponge mattress besides a few items of clothing. We plan to be gone only two days. There are twelve of us going on this voyage. No moon so it is pitch black as we file along the path, one behind the other, each carrying something on his head or in his hand or both. Marion flicks on the torch whenever the way gets too rough and broken. Cannot break a leg now. Not out here in the middle of the night between the forest and the deep blue sea!

An hour later and we are finally sea borne. The wind is gentle but enough to spread the sails. A sliver of a moon has appeared and the stars twinkle above us. The boat we are in is twenty-four feet long. We have each been assigned our nook with the stern end going to Marion and me. Our luggage is tucked behind us, making a fine back-rest. The three operating the sail boat are from the Islands and are anxious to take us there.

The pace is slow. Then suddenly the wind is in our face as we draw abreast of Sigulu Island. It has switched direction hours ahead of schedule! The sails become useless and we are forced to dock near the west end of the island where one of our churchs is located. The plan was to stop in here tomorrow on our return voyage. To try and paddle the remaining forty-five miles south-west to Lolui would be suicidal. We could never survive facing into the high waves which are out there in the deep. Our boatsmen inform us that they have lost their cargo whenever they tried to sail winds which were contrary. It is light when we dock on Sigulu. The village, Namugongo is only a stone's throw away so we do not have far to walk. The Christians are not expecting us, but manage to make us welcome. Water is brought and we take our baths behind a raised sheet of plastic tied to a couple of trees. Then all of us find a place to catch up on some much needed sleep. Marion and I are given one of the huts. Soon I discover tiny ants are biting me. We must have laid our mattress on top of their nest.

We cannot set sail until the winds are again blowing from the north-east which means we will be here until midnight. Marion has brought along her box of dawa and is quite busy all afternoon treating the sick. Margaret assists her. Meanwhile Francis baptizes twenty-four converts in the lake. The waves tug at them, threatening to sweep them away into the lake. Watching the waters pound the shore-line I can believe that we surely would perish should we be caught out in the middle of that vast lake. I preach in the evening service and twenty-two accept Christ.

After a late meal, Marion and I lie down on our mattress in a grass roofed hut, at about ten to await the call to depart. Not long after extinguishing the lantern a rat scurries across Marion's face! She whacks at it and hits me instead. I re-light the lantern and leave it burning to discourage them from moving about so freely. We can see them peeking at us from every corner. That must have been a rat under the mattress as something moved when Marion lay on it! She had gotten to bed before I did. I wonder if it was the same rat which just startled her?

We are awakened at three o'clock in the morning and in half an hour we are in the boat. The wind is not cooperative. In fact, quite contrary. It could not make up it's mind which way to blow. And at times none at all! The sails are switched from side to side. Paddles are put into use. But our progress is slow, as if we are anchored to Sigulu Island. When the wind settles in the south, the crew aim the boat for Sagitu Island to the west. They can get some help from the sails going in this direction. Though the boat handles the cross current quite well, Ephraim and another passenger are soon sea-sick.

As we draw near to Sagitu we swing to the south in order to make Lolui Island. The wind is now coming from the south-west. With the paddles assisting the sails we draw nearer to the elusive island. Skirting Sagitu, our church on this island is pointed out to us. There is a church on another island further north which we can see against the horizon called Vumba. But our rendezvous with the islanders is scheduled to be on Lolui, the largest of the three.

At eleven o'clock, we finally land on their beach. A voyage that should have taken four hours at the most takes seven and a half! This is the hour we should be preparing to return to catch the winds before they increase in volume and the waves become too high. By the signs in the sky there will be rain squalls out at sea this afternoon. We make the decision then to stay the day until the winds are favourable on the morrow. This makes the islanders happy as they did not want us to leave so soon. Out here schedules are made and re-made. Not only are the winds contrary but so are schedules.

We are made welcome in someone's compound. Bath water is prepared for us. The sail is hung across cassava plants and we take turns in huddling behind it for a much needed wash. We soon learn there are no latrines on the island. The reason given is that the ground is too rocky to dig. So a "jembe" (hoe) is available to use when the need arises. But by the grapevine we hear that the Luo, who are the majority of the population on these islands, do not believe in latrines. If the woman or man uses it, then pregnancy will not take place. Therefore they simply are not dug.

Marion uses up all her medicine this afternoon. She and Margaret are swamped with patients. Many youngsters are covered with scabies. She discovers cases of bilharzia, something we have not seen since the days of Tanzania where most of the Wambugwe suffered from this disease. The need for cleanliness is great on Lolui. We are asked to open a clinic here. And surely they need one desperately. But before that can take place a boat must be gotten. One with sails would be more practical than one with a motor. Such as the one we came in on, would suffice. To sail when the winds are not contrary.

Before retiring tonight there is a service where ten are prayed for after my message. The singing goes on and we are ready for bed. But alas! We discover our companions for the night will again be rats! As soon as the light has been extinguished they are everywhere. Dirt drops down onto my face as they hurry along the edge above me. I am lying with my face too near the wall. They peer down at us in the light of the torch. In the dark one brushes the side of my face and arm as it scampers to destinations unknown. The owner of the house has fish, which are smaller than sardines, in a container stacked in a corner. They knock that down. Marion feverishly searches for a match to relight the candle. Digging around in her basket she finally comes up, after several attempts, with a packet. The light dispels them and they quieten down enough to allow us to get some sleep. It is one-thirty in the morning.

Get up at light. Tired but glad to see the dawn. Rats are no favorite of mine! All is ready at eight o'clock to embark. But it showers some and we are delayed for two hours. Then, at ten we commence loading the boat. Singing "Tembea na Yesu" we launch out into the deep. The wind is agreeable. We sway with the swelling waves. Our pace quickens the further we get from land. Looking back I see the sea attempting to gulp down the vessel repeatedly, but the winds keep us just out of reach. We ride ahead of the tempestous sea. I am enjoying the return voyage immensely!

We pass through the edge of a cloud of insects which resemble mosquitoes only a bit smaller. They cling to the sails and get into our hair forcing Marion to cover her head with a cloth. Ever since we have been on this voyage clouds of these insects have been spotted against the horizon in each direction. They ride the currents to cross from island to island. There are billions of them in each cloud! It is quite a sight to behold when one of the clouds suddenly spiral heaven-wards. An up-draft must have caught them. Surely countless of them must perish during these pilgrimages.

Cruising along side Sigulu Island which is twelve miles

in length, we spot a monitar lizard on a rock. And then we are in the straight between Bugana Island and Sigulu. No time to stop at Budama to visit our church. I had hoped to see it. The church on the north end of Bugana we have visited twice. Took Mark, our son, and the Kellseys from Canada there on our first voyage. Tim and Colleen accompanied me on the second one. To enter we passed with the boat through the reeds which eventually opened to reveal a Shangri-la. There above us was a village nestled against tall trees. They have literally hacked out a settlement in the jungle. A sight to behold, truly!

At three in the afternoon, we dock at Busiro amid shouts of welcome and songs of joy. We all praise the Lord together for returning us safely. Since yesterday evening when we were scheduled to return, the Christians have been concerned. They know of too many who have lost their lives while sailing when winds were contrary. God has been with us and we thank Him, for treating us to a beautiful return voyage. It could not have been more splendid or scenic. The five hours blew by quickly.

There are many hands to carry everyone's luggage back to the church. We are glad for that, for the sun bore down on us during our whole time at sea. Ready for a cold drink and a shower. The latter I get after we arrive at the church. But the former is far from cold. It is hot tea which we are served before we load our vehicle, which fared well during our absence, and re-trace our way back home.

# Chapter Seventeen
# The Harvest is Plentiful But . . .

This is my last safari up country before my faithful companion and I part company. Marion and I will be leaving for our furlough next month and the one who has made sure I reached my destination, trekking to and fro will no longer assist me. We have roughed it together for 105,000 kilometers over some of the roughest roads imaginable. Through it all my Nissan Patrol has never left me stranded. When we received it three and a half years ago, Marion and I had lovingly laid our hands on it and committed it to the Lord, asking Him to bless it in His service. I named it "Silver Wings." It had to have wings in order to get there before and after dark. Or, home before too late so that Marion would not begin to worry. I have nothing but praise for my silver wagon which has helped transport the gospel without failure.

Ever since coming to Uganda four years ago my aim has been to carry the gospel up to Karamoja in northeastern Uganda. Then year after year slipped by without my dream becoming reality. There was always something standing in the way. Either a war, or just too involved planting churches in other districts which were opening up to us at a rapid pace. The longer I waited the more difficult it became. Will I make it to this fierce tribe before I go on furlough? I must!

The Karamojong are still clinging to their former way of life. They have not kept up with the progress of civilization as have other tribes in Uganda. Their life is cattle and believe they all belong to them. It does not matter in whose custody they are today, for eventually all cattle will belong to them. The Karamojong sincerely believe this. And this is what makes them dangerous. Even more so than in yester-years. With automatic weapons in their possession they are a foe very difficult to conquer. They strike terror into the bravest of men.

The warriors are fearless. Before striking a district or village, they send word that they are coming on the morrow. When they arrive there is no resistance for all have fled. Even the soldiers at the road-blocks have melted into the bush. Reinforcements always have the habit of appearing after the raid which often will take days in itself. But then who wants to tackle these men who run through brush as if there was none? Who are masters at ambushes and never leave any dead! If you want to keep living, flee for your life, or you are no more.

I am thrilled that finally the Nissan Patrol is pointing in the direction of Karamoja. Due to the danger of this trip, Marion has remained at home. Rufus, Ephraim and Francis Makosia are with me. Francis has been up there and arrangements have been made for our stay. While in Karamoja he visited Moroto and fifteen manyattas where he was received warmly. So we expect no major problem or setback. But one never knows. Our lives are in His hands.

Entering North Bugisu we come across hundreds on the road returning to their homes from where they fled just two weeks ago. How long will it take before the Karamojong raiders strike again? We halt at Bunangaka to enquire of our district chairman, who has returned, about the condition of our churches. For back in Mbale we met one pastor who informed us that nearly fifty Christians have fled to his home only a few miles out of Mbale. He has been feeding them since. I promised him assistance on my return from Karamoja.

The chairman confirms the exodus of the residents from North Bugisu. But that many are now in the process of returning. Where else can they live? This is home, no matter how dangerous it may become. There are crops they must attend to if they expect a harvest. He has left his wife and children outside the troubled area. They will move back when peace has been established. Others are doing the same.

The settlement Atari, near the Sebei border is vacant. No one has returned as yet. We discover that it is the same in Sebei. Passing through the three villages where we have churches we discover them empty. No life any where, except in the last one where there is a road-block and a few onlookers. The inhabitants have fled onto the slopes of Mount Elgon where we have several more congregations. This tribe borders the Karamojong and have felt the brunt of their attacks for as long as they care to remember.

I could not help but remember as we passed the second village Seretyo, the child we prayed for on our visit there some time ago. We were just departing, having concluded our service which was under the tree when a villager halted us. Would we come to treat a child who was dying. All we had along was dawa for malaria. "Go and pray for the child," Marion had said. And so Francis and I had walked to the hut to inspect the child's condition. Entering the dark hut I find the child, who is still an infant, dehydrated and lying on a cow skin. Smoke is curling lazily from a gourd containing certain weeds. Fetishes are tied to the baby's hand and around the throat and waist. There are other signs which tell us that the medicine man has been consulted.

Before praying for the child, the parents are told to clear out all the paraphernalia. Christ must have pre-eminence I tell them. When the conditions are met we lay on hands and pray for deliverance. The evil spirits are cast out of the hut and the illness bound in Jesus' name. All the signs are there that the child will die unless the Lord performs a miracle. Returning to the vehicle, I spotted an expectant mother. She is not yet in her teens, Marion had been told by some by-standers!

What did happen to that child? I ask Francis. He goes on to tell me that on his following visit he found the child healed! Praise the Lord! He performed a miracle. The parents are so thankful that we had taken time that day to call in and pray for the child, Francis says. They are grateful for the missionary's prayers. So the child is alive and with her parents up on the slopes of Mount Elgon somewhere at this moment.

Crossing the Kelim Creek, we find ourselves in Karamoja. It is wild country. There should be game here. Francis says there used to be plenty but now-a-days they are found further down. "In years gone by Europeans used to hunt in this area," I am told by him. The mountains that stand alone spread out across the flat-land. They appear majestic and secretive. What stories they must hold! Smaller outcrops are visible as well. Francis informs us there are caves in many of them. One of them contains a large snake. Had we time he would take us to the cave. "It is not far away," he chimes. I wonder.

The lights on the dash go out. We are in the middle of nowhere. Not a soul is in sight. I switch off the engine, but the motor keeps running. Put it into gear and stall it. Lifting up the hood, I find several wires loose near the battery. The connections have been eaten away by acid. Half an hour later I have the wiring patched sufficiently to put us back on the road.

We are now in territory where the Suk from Kenya often attack the Karamojong for their cattle. That is probably why at Namalu one of the soldiers manning the road-block is grumpy. Must have had a bad night. After peeking into our luggage we are on the move again. But not for long, for there is another road-block. Many Karamojong standing around. Several women beg for a lift to some destination down the road. No room. So they are refused. They rattle on in their language but we fail to understand them. Their smell reminds me of the Masai who are cattle keepers as well, but live in Kenya and Tanzania. They too believe all cattle belong to them.

Coming around a bend we spot a lone Karamojong warrior. He is driving five head of cattle and was ready to cross the road when we interrupted him. He swerves them to the side his automatic weapon on the ready. We keep moving, trying to appear uninterested as much as possible. He is driving his portion of the herd raided from Sebei and North Bugisu. Had we a soldier in the vehicle with us, the warrior would have shot him and maybe us as well, Francis tells us. Fortunately, the soldier had disembarked at the Namalu road-block whom we had assisted when a group of them stopped us for help several miles back. That was close!

Twice we come across Karamojong transporting huge loads on their backs. Their divy of the loot. We were not to witness this as well? Then we enter a section of Karamoja where there is no village for twenty or more miles. It is warrior country, Francis says. The landscape is bushy, containing many gullies. An ideal place for their rendezvous. Dik-dik dart across the road now and then as we push on to Moroto. Plenty of guinea fowl who scurry out of the way always in time.

We reach Moroto before six o'clock. It is snuggled in the arms of a mountain by the same name. The district head-quarters are located here. Upon arrival we report in at the police station which is manned by a lone female. She is one of our Christians here in town and we find ourselves in her home for the evening meal. Her husband is a retired officer. Before long others gather and I find myself sharing the Word of God with them. It is late before I turn in for the night. It has been a very long day. Had gotten up at six this morning in order to get an early start.

Before heading out to the manyattas I take my vehicle to the Roman Catholic Mission for fuel as it is the only place with any at all. While there, I have the job I did yesterday on the electrical wiring, redone. Watching him work I wonder who the amateur really is as I see no improvement on the way I had done it.

Several miles out of Moroto, we pull up to our first manyatta. It does not take long and we are surrounded by the occupants. Children coated in dust appear from everywhere, all of them naked except for sandals on their feet and the girls wearing tiny loin pieces made from goat skin. The "wazee" (old men) who have been squatting in the shade of the tree now stand to greet us. Their blankets which are draped around their shoulders fail to hide their nakedness as they shake our hands. They are very old and the eyes of some are infected. I have noticed several children with the same disease. It is easily spread by the flies which abound in this environment.

The women appear next on the scene. Maidens have hair designs so different from those seen elsewhere. Instead of leaving them to grow and then braiding them into rows as others do, they cut them all off leaving but several rows of short hair for a design. A lot easier! Instead of beads they prefer wire circling their necks. There are rolls of them on most. Ears have several holes pierced into them. The older women court the wooden peg in their lower lip as do the wazee. It is for beauty comes the reply, when I ask why they have it. Finally the young bucks, who are not out on a raid, sidle into view. Their black cloths slung over their shoulders fail to reach far enough to cover their buttocks and elsewhere.

We discuss with the wazee our purpose to share the gospel with them. That is fine with them but what about assisting them with food. A meager supply of sorghum remains and they are eating but once a day. I ask their spokesman whether any aid group has been supplying them with rations. The reply is negative. Why is that? How many more manyattas are there in such a condition? "And what about clothes for our naked bodies," the old man says sweeping his arm around to indicate his people.

I return the conversation to our coming here regularly with the gospel. Could we meet under that nearby tree each Sunday to talk about God and the gospel of Jesus Christ? The tree we are grouped under is too near the manyatta. The wazee huddle together to decide our future with them. Squatting on their haunches they give full attention to one who is their medicine man or diviner as he is now slapping his sandals on the ground. Three times they strike and then he tosses them down. Which way will they land, is the question? Ah, the matter is settled. We are accepted, for the scandals point towards the tree I have chosen instead of the one in front of the manyatta.

We must move on to another manayatta. Before leaving I pull out a bunch of bananas I have brought along. The children and young women grasp them from my hands before I can choose which ones should receive them! Informing them we will be back tomorrow, Sunday, we head for our second manyatta. We leave behind at least one hundred and fifty Karamojong who will need our assistance in food and clothes if we are to be effective with the gospel.

Sharing the gospel is often more than preaching and teaching. Were it just that, it would make it much simpler in carrying out the great commission. But what do you do when you stand in a village where the only food they have will feed them just one more week? That is if they ration it to one meal a day. In another village water is miles away in a muddy hole that is shared with livestock and is rapidly drying up. Then you are in a village that has recently been looted by rebels. The houses are empty and the grain bins smashed. What do you do then with the lump in your throat and the ache in your heart and the tears that push their way through, no matter how hard you try to hide them? "Am I my brothers' keeper?"

I can either say yes to that question, or I can refuse. The deciding factor for me is this portion of Scripture, "For I was hungry and you gave me something to eat, I was thirsty and you gave me something to drink . . . , I needed clothes and you clothed me, I was sick and you looked after me . . . , whatever you did for one of the least of these brothers of mine, you did for me." (Matthew 25:35, 36, 40). By the way, it was Jesus who said that! The One who gave us the great commission.

At the second manyatta we discover the same condition. Only there are more of them here. We meet under a tree between several manyattas, each a short distance away. They want us to come and teach them, as well as help them. The chief is their spokesman. He shakes my hand profusely, lifting it high and holding it there. I share with them the need to worship God and to obey Him by accepting Christ. Peter is interpreting for me. He is a Karamojong, a young man Francis found on his last safari. He has accepted Christ and is eager to serve Him.

Before we leave, we give a T.E.E. book and Bible to a young man who has been chosen by the group to be their teacher in the Word. Then we are on our way to a third meeting place that Francis and Peter arranged for us to attend. There are two manyattas here, just one hundred feet apart. Must be three hundred Karamojong residing in this place. Many women are away catching flying ants. They are part of their diet during the rainy season. Others are returning with bundles of firewood on their backs.

We take time to enter one of the manyattas and visit a few homes on the inside. Before we get to them though we must bend low down to get through the opening in the thorn fence surrounding the manyatta. Once inside I am surprised to find there is no resemblance to the Masai boma. It is not open throughout with huts alongside the stockade. Instead it is sectioned off with a family in each portion. There is more privacy here than with the Masai.

Rain is commencing to fall. It has been approaching

from the south side of Mount Moroto for some time. I must leave now as the trail we came in on is not an all-weather road. Had to use the four-wheel drive all the way. We manage to reach Moroto without any problem. In the afternoon I am busy teaching on the church to the group gathered here in town. Not too many, but enough to start a church.

Sunday morning finds us returning to the three manyattas we visited yesterday. With me I have four bags of posho which I purchased last night. One sack is distributed to the first group. Children are treated to biscuits bought for that purpose. All goes well with the diviner in charge of the receiving lines. There is no queue jumping. Marvellous! More infected eyes are treated. We did quite a few yesterday at all three manyattas. Thankful Marion stuck in several items of medicine, especially the eye ointment.

At the second and third manyattas the distribution of the food is chaotic! The only thing we can control to a certain extent is the giving out of the biscuits to the children. But with the posho we have a battle on our hands. Even the chief cannot control the women. It takes only a few minutes and there is queue jumping. Then, before we know it, the ones in charge of passing out the flour are surrounded by hands with containers. I thought, I will solve the problem by standing beside the posho. Oh yeah! My not-so-clean-anymore shirt testifies of nearly getting mobbed several times. Peter, Francis and I keep sliding the sack away from them and marking off a new line with the stick which they are not to cross if they want to receive flour. We could have saved our breath for the rule is again broken a minute later.

The food is far too little! It always is. Had we come with ten times as much, there still would be late comers who would miss out. But we did what we could. Came with as much as there was room for in the vehicle. Thus we were able to minister to them in word and deed. We left exhausted but satisfied. Openings have been established for the gospel. There is a leader at each manyatta who has been enrolled in our ministerial program. The first book, "Following Jesus," with an English Bible for himself, plus one in Karimojong to read to the congregation.

Am so glad I was able to come and see for myself the life they live here in Karamoja. True, there are many warriors who are cold and deadly, but I also discovered those who are warm and friendly. There is such an opportunity here in this district, to reap a harvest of souls if we will only deny ourselves of some plenty and share it with them. It is much easier to complain of the lack of funds, instead of praying that the needs of the open fields and waiting souls be met. But God does hear prayer and is faithful to supply every need.

"When He saw the crowds, He had compassion on them, because they were harassed and helpless, like sheep without a shepherd. Then He said to His disicples, "The harvest is plentiful but the workers are few. Ask the Lord of the harvest, therefore, to send out workers into His harvest field.' " (Matthew 9:36-38).

# Chapter Eighteen
## To Regions Beyond

Africa has been my life ever since I was old enough to read. The lands in the dark continent fascinated me. God so lovingly has granted me that permission to see many parts of this world I read and re-read about during my younger years. Not just to visit for a day or a week, but to travel in-land, live among the inhabitants, eat their food and experience their hardships. To listen to their stories and learn their beliefs. After sharing Christ with them, to see Him change the lives of those who accept Him. I will always be grateful to Him for opening the door for me to go to regions beyond with the precious gospel.

From Tanzania, we moved to Kenya. Then to Uganda. While here in Uganda, we come in contact with Mianitse Kyambali of Zaire rather by accident at the Kenya/Uganda border in August 1983. He was stranded. The officials on the Kenya side would not allow him passage as he had no visa. So I gave him fare money to return to Kampala. While attending the World Conference in

Nairobi, I was asked whether I would visit the churches in Zaire who were interested in associating with the Church of God. Upon my return, Mianitse and I discussed at length the background to the group in eastern Zaire situated mainly in Kivu province. The result was that Paul Hutchins, Marion and I make a trip to Goma in March, 1984.

The safari is made in our Nissan. We pass through the border at Ishasha into Zaire, formerly called Belgian Congo. The road that greets us is a real test for our new vehicle. We swim through mire two and three feet deep. Before reaching Goma we find ourselves in the dark shadows of a jungle. There are gorillas up on the volcanos to our one side and pygmies in the jungle to the other. After exiting from the heavy vegetation, we encounter lava. It is everywhere! Volcanos have erupted in the past belching fire and brimstone upon the dwellers below. The stream of molten rock reached as far south as Goma on the shore of Lake Kivu.

One volcano is still active and we are told that it erupted back in 1979 killing many as lava buried roads and villages. An eerie sight to a stranger but a common one to the local folks. When will it again spew forth the venom? Every how many years did they say? Not for a few more years, I believe.

Will not forget the lodging we are taken to while in Goma. There is no running water and an out-house we do not enter unless positively necessary. The nook where we take our showers is anything but private. Something like the bedrooms where we can hear the persons talking two doors down. We soon learn to whisper or mumble. Fortunately no one understands English as French and Swahili are spoken here. Our communication is in the latter.

Twenty miles west of Goma is Sake where Mianitse lives. Here we preach to a large crowd out-doors which numbers over five hundred. The village is literally built on a lava bed. You are walking on cinders constantly, or stumbling over lava rocks. A few trees peek through wherever they are able to find crevices. To the west lie their shambas on the green and fertile hills where the villagers dig and graze their livestock. Up there and beyond are churches which wish to be a part of us.

I return to Zaire a year later passing through Rwanda this time. Found the roads much better on this route. Marion sits this one out, but Paul is with me. Things are being worked out for their acceptance. At Sake we hold a seminar where the pastors have gathered for classes. Then in October, 1986, I fly there for my third visit. Donald Williams, the Associate Secretary of the Missionary Board, is accompanying me. The final touches are made so that the church is legally registered. Discover that the active volcano erupted in May and molten lava spilled within a few miles of Sake.

It is May, 1987. I am here for my final visit. Flew into Goma in a Missionary Aviation Fellowship twin-engined fifteen-seater from Nairobi. Enroute it made stops at Mwanza and Bukavu. I enjoyed the flight. Mianitse takes me to the Catholic guesthouse where Paul and I stayed on my second safari. Here the Christians from the congregation in Goma bring me food to eat as they did on the previous occasion. This annoys the European sister and when she keeps complaining about their presence, Mianitse moves me to a low rate hotel nearby.

Here the management does not mind visitors in my room, nor food brought to me. The room is bare, except for two cots, so a table and stool are asked to be brought. Sprawling out on my cot, when finally alone, I discover it has fleas. I am bitten by them in short order. Lying here I notice brownish rings on the ceiling where rain has leaked onto it from holes in the roof. I count twenty of them! One resembles a fourteen inch tire and rim, with one exception. Not the right shade. They have placed a watchman at my door for the night. He is quite noisy. Does a lot of coughing, mumbles about something and chews dry maize. Sounds like a dog crackling a bone.

Because of a time change, I keep awakening at five o'clock. Others are doing the same as I hear vehicles moving about early in the morning. In the evening the Christians wish to visit while I am ready for sleep. All day long I am either teaching or preaching. Make arrangements for the pastors to enroll in the T.E.E. course. Mianitse reports there are presently one hundred and forty-three churches in Zaire with 5,137 believers attending. Praise the Lord for this growth which has occurred in the last three years. There are supposed to be eighty-six more churches in Shaba and Kasai provinces further south and west, but I am unable to find time to go there to visit them. Met their delegation twice while in Zambia. They found it nearer to meet me there.

While here in Goma, I am transported back and forth to Sake in vehicles of all sorts and models. But they have one thing in common—they must be pushed before they start. Most of them have no headlights that work so we travel by faith after dark. One in the group comments, "That driver has little faith," as we see another vehicle approaching us with only one light. In other words, if both lights are working then you do not have faith. And if no lights, then you really are travelling by faith. He is not joking!

The shocks and springs are non-existant, and the only cushion on the back seat is the seat of your pants. They believe you must sit in the back. After all does not every V.I.P. sit there? The driver keeps switching off the engine to conserve fuel. Whether he succeeds is debatable as he has to rev the motor to gain sufficient speed to coast, and then to accelerate again to pick up speed after having coasted to a near stand still.

I am here in Zaire a week and am exhausted many a night. Pray for strength and He keeps reviving me. They do not realize that they are changing off in their visiting me, coming in relays, and therefore get a break. But I am on the receiving end for them all! I make it and meet the M.A.F. plane which flies me back to Nairobi again via Bukavu and Mwanza.

*     *     *

I meet Esron Twagiramungu on my first visit to Zaire. He introduces himself to me and says that he has several churches in Rwanda which wish to affiliate with us. So, on my second journey to Zaire which I take through Rwanda, I see some of the pastors at Gisenyi. The road we travel on winds through and over beautiful green hills which are terraced into small shambas from the bottom to the top.

Rwanda is small in size therefore the most densely populated country in Africa. Within her border dwell the Batutsi, the tallest tribe in Africa. They are also found in Burundi, Rwanda's neighbour to the south. Both of these countries, along with Tanzania, made up German East Africa at the turn of the twentieth century.

Esron accompanies Mianitse on his trips to visit me here in Kampala. We discuss the work at length and pray together for God to have His way. It is on the trip with Donald Williams that we see the officials about registration of the Church when we stop at Kigali, the capital.

From here a taxi drives us to Gisenyi. He takes us around hair-pin curves which would do justice to any East African rally driver! We are thankful for the break when he is asked to halt midway Ruhengeri and Gisenyi for a service at a village called Jenda. Here six hundred and eighty have gathered under the hot mid-day sun to meet us and to hear from us. Pray for many after delivering the message.

At Gisenyi more officials are visited. The pastors have assembled and the Word is shared with them. Preach again in the service as well with many seeking Christ. A good start has been made here. It should blossom out now. When I return in May of this year, I meet with the pastors and church leaders again. This time for two days. As in Zaire, the pastors here will be taking the T.E.E. studies. Esron reports the work has grown to ninety-two churches with 2,998 Christians. Praise the Lord!

*       *       *

A year ago, I began receiving some letters from London Sikazwe, a brother in Zambia who invites me to come and meet with Christians who wish to fellowship with the Church of God. As the Associate Secretary of the Missionary Board was coming out around this time, a visit is planned with the group. Thus, in October, Donald and I find ourselves in Zambia. It is a profitable meeting and decisions are made to register the church with us. Many gather for the classes and services at Kitwe. Some of the best choirs I have ever heard, I now hear singing here in Zambia. Their harmony is magnificent!

Before leaving Zambia, while praying for the work in Central Africa, the Lord burdens my heart for it. I am ready to rise to the challenge. Silver and gold have I none, but what I have I give to thee, O Lord. My life, my all.

Three months later Marion accompanies me on my second safari to Zambia. Before travelling on to Kitwe, we go down to Livingstone and visit the world's most majestic water-falls. David Livingstone the missionary who wandered all through these parts, when he first viewed it, named the falls after Queen Victoria. To the local inhabitants it is Musi-o-Tunya (the smoke that thunders). There are no words to describe the greatness of these falls. Victoria Falls surpasses them all! You are gripped with awe as you stand on the brink, the spray soaking you to the bone, gazing at this colossal handi-work of God!

We attend their services and meetings. The choirs sing for us and again I am greatly impressed by their harmony. They are always in tune! Purchase T.E.E. books and Bibles for the T.E.E. program which the pastors are going to receive commencing now. Marion and I ride back to Lusaka in a bus. We pass through a few road-blocks but they are mild in comparison with those in Uganda. It is a five hour trip.

We spend several nights in Lusaka on the compound of a missionary couple from Canada. Marion is awakened at four o'clock one morning by strange noises coming from outside the cabin. Sounded like someone walking about. Twigs snapped a few times. As she peeks out of the window, she spies two men at the vehicle on the yard. She promptly awakens me with a whisper, "Stan, thieves are attempting to steal Kurtz's vehicle." It takes me only a second to come fully awake. Nothing snaps me alert as quickly as a whisper.

The window Marion is peering through is right above me. Straightening up I take a peek as well. There they are alright. One is standing beside the door which is ajar, while the second is behind the steering wheel. Then we hear the starter begin to grind. Again and again. The engine fails to start. I rap on the window a few times. Do they carry guns? Are the thieves any different here in Zambia?

The man outside the vehicle stares in our direction. Must have found it hard to distinguish us in the dark. The man inside tries to start the engine again. It almost caught that time. I rap once more on the window. This time the driver looks our way. They exchange a few words and then walk slowly out of the yard. The two watch dogs made no sound during the whole time! Had it not been for Marion's watchfulness, the vehicle would surely have gotten stolen.

I had wanted so much to make a trip to Malawi while here in Zambia on this safari, to make contact with some Christians there. But time was not on our side. Another day, the Lord willing.

I return alone for my third visit in May of this year. Discover that the work is progressing satisfactorily. There are thirty-five congregations established containing 5,752 Christians. Pastors have begun studying their T.E.E. books. I meet with them and share about Christ and the Church. At Kitwe we gather under the open sky in their church building which does not have a roof as yet. The sun makes one wish that it would have one. Over three hundred are present in the service where many seek prayer after the message.

I am glad it was possible for me to be here once more before going on furlough. The leadership needs guidance and instructions. Travelling from place to place is done in vehicles which are more mobile than those in Zaire. Eat in homes with the Christians and listen to their needs. While at Lusaka, I preach in two different churches. The church wants us to come and stay in Zambia.

I thank the Lord for allowing me to see first hand the regions beyond Uganda during the past four years. Will I be seeing them again? God only knows.

# Chapter Nineteen
# The Tarnished Pearl

Uganda lies in the heart of Africa. It is surrounded by five countries, namely, Kenya, Tanzania, Rwanda, Zaire and Sudan. Cradled between Mount Elgon on the east side and the Ruwenzori Mountains on the west, the equator slices through its southern half. From Lake Victoria which it straddles, flows the longest river in the world. the Nile begins its journey at Jinja and keeps flowing, inspite of the hot sands of Sudan and Egypt, until it enters the Mediterranean Sea.

In its 236,000 square kilometers exist fifteen million Ugandans made up of thirty-six or more tribes. Most of these are Bantu, with the remainder divided between the Nilotics and the Nilo-Hamitics. Surprisingly 32% still are animist, clinging to their traditional beliefs. Only 8% say they are Muslim, while the remaining 60% are equally divided between the Roman Catholics and the Protestants states a Bible Society report.

The first Europeans to visit Uganda were the explorers who arrived in 1844 as well as Arab traders. Stanley, after locating Livingstone in Tanganyika, also traveled extensively in the Lake Victoria region. He visited the Baganda king, the Kabaka, on several occasions. In 1890 Uganda came under British influence and soon missionaries traveled to this land-locked country.

Uganda gained its independence in 1962. The first president was the king of the ancient kingdom of Buganda, but he was supplanted by his prime minister a few years later. In 1971 Milton Obote was himself replaced in a military coup by General Idi Amin. His dictatorial rule ended in 1979 and a year later Obote was back for a second time. But political rivalry and tribalism continued. General Tito Okello became the head of state in 1985 after a successful military coup. However six months later he is toppled by the guerrilla leader Yoweri Museveni who is the current president of Uganda.

It is reported that 500,000 died during Amin's regime and another 600,000 perished under the hand of Obote's ruthless soldiers. How many have been killed needlessly since then? No one really knows. When life is cheap who cares about statistics! Mass graves and occupants of entire villages massacred testify a lack of reverance for human life. As I watch youngsters nine years of age in army fatigues toting automatic weapons, my heart is saddened. What is the future for this generation, and the next? Lads who carried our baskets at the market now carry an AK-47.

Kampala is spread out over numerous hills, one of them is Mengo. On its crest I have stood beside the graves of those pioneer missionaries who ventured out from England before the turn of the century. One is that of Mackay, another that of Hannington who was speared to death by the Kabaka's warriors. His last words were: "Tell the Kabaka I die for Uganda." I stand in awe of their courage and dedication! May I be found faithful onto the end as well.

Winston Churchill on his visit to Uganda called it the pearl of Africa. That pearl is tarnished though. It is very bloody. Many of the first converts to Christianity were put to death by burning them as one would firewood. Blood was spilt then and it continues to be spilled. Yet in the midst of all this shedding of blood, many Ugandans want peace and tranquility. It is these who are accepting Jesus Christ as we carry the gospel to the villages throughout the bleeding and tarnished countryside.

The Word of God must continue to go forth as many still adhere to evil practices inspite of Christianity entering a century ago. Drunkenness abounds in the villages and in the city. Pombi, or waragi as it is called in Uganda, is readily concocted from bananas, millet and just about any other local grains. A social gathering is never with out its pombi. To give it up completely, the person must be converted. I have witnessed Christ change many a drunkard from his old life of sin. The message of salvation is his only hope.

Because of man's desire to be head of a large family, and the fact that women outnumber men in Uganda due to the wars, polygamy is widely practiced. It is culturally accepted by all the tribes. Many women in fact approve of polygamy. They appreciate the company and see nothing wrong with having another person to help with the work. It is not an indignity to be one of several wives, and may even insist that her husband take another wife to assist her. No woman wishes to be looked upon as having something wrong with her. Therefore polygamy is inevitable if all women are to get married.

The man is to abstain from sex with his wife while she is expecting and continue to keep away while she is suckling the child which may take two or more years. In the Baganda and Banyoro traditions they abstain until the child is weaned. The belief is that if they do not, breast milk will disappear and the baby will die due to the lack of a healthy diet. The result is that many husbands turn to polygamy.

In the compound of a polygamist I have noted a hut for each wife where she resides with her children. The husband, in this case a Teso, has his own hut and visits his wives only to have sex. The food is brought to him in his own dwelling. In Bunyoro I learned the husband stays in his wives' huts, visiting each one by rotation. He may spend a week or more with each wife. While there she is expected to cook and care for him. In a few other polygamous societies where a husband cannnot afford to erect a separate hut for each wife, one building will house them all. Each woman will have her own room and cooking utensils. They take turns cooking and caring for the husband.

Inspite of living on friendly terms with each other, wives will quarrel and show jealousy, especially when the husband dies. Whose child should be the heir? As a rule, however, wives are expected to respect the senior or first wife's wishes. It is not uncommon to find co-wives accusing each other of doing evil. If one of them stays childless while another bears children, the barren woman will accuse the other of sorcery. There will be persecution and even murder as a result.

A polygamist has to be rich if he is to succeed for he must provide his wives equally with clothes and cooking utensils. He cannot favour one above the other without expecting trouble. He must treat all children equally as well. If he does not there is strife on the compound. He sees less of his children than does a monogamist, since each mother tends to live in an isolated circle within the family. The father is a stranger to his children. Half-brothers quarrel over the inheritance and over rank. Jealousy amongst sons can be more serious than between wives! Many tragedies occur in the villages where polygamy is being practiced.

Polygamy also creates a problem among the young men who wish to marry. They find that older rich polygamous husbands have diminished the supply of females. And should the young man be poor, he will not find a wife at all. Or, he may end up marrying an older woman, most likely a widow, for whom the dowry is very little. Often he is caught courting one of the younger wives of a polygamist who finds herself dissatisfied and is seeking her own pleasures elsewhere.

Will they ever leave this practice? With Christ they can, and are moving from a polygamous to a monogamous society. But it has been an uphill struggle all the way. Another practice which existed in the Old Testament among God's people, as polygamy, was circumcision. This rite is still practiced among the Bagisu and the Sebei in eastern Uganda. In Bugisu it is performed every even year. Old customary dancing before the ceremony is still observed. The youth sing, blow whistles, dance and beat drums. They trot in procession from hut to hut chanting and jingling their bells. This merry-making commences a month or more before the initiation is performed which is usually before the year ends.

An enclosure is erected for the circumcision ceremony. Or it may simply be in the courtyard of the parents as it was when I observed the ritual take place. The candidates for circumcision know where to stand upon entering the selected site now packed with onlookers. After jumping a few times each initiate must now stand still to await the operators. The father, or guardian, in the meantime is smearing the boy's torso with juices from inside of a goat's stomach. Not far from me stands a small shrine with an internal organ from that same goat sticking on a pole. It is for the ancestral spirit.

The operator pulls the foreskin forward all the way and cuts it off with his special knife. The piece is then collected by the father and buried in a secret place unknown to all, including the witches. It is then that I notice the meat on the pole has vanished! Did the spirit of his ancestor really take it? I am determined to be more alert next time. And I am. Just as the foreskin is severed, and all eyes are on the initiate, I spy the mother snatch the morsel from its perch!

During the operation the boy, who is in his middle teens, must not flinch or show any sign of fear. Even the twitching of an eyelid is considered as cowardice. (I noticed at the last place the mother had to slap the boy's thighs several times when she observed them quivering.) After the operation is done, the boys jump a few times to show their joy and courage. Then they sit on stools and cloths are draped over their shoulders. Before long the blood commences to clot and the youth, now men, are ushered into a special hut by their fathers. Attendants care for them till the wounds have healed. The whole village has already broken out into dancing and drinking which carries on all night. The new initiates have attained manhood and are now full members of their clan.

It is a shameful thing should one of them show fear and collapse. His parents will feel let down and will hate him for it. Children will mock and tease him until the incident is forgotten years later. A boy who is unwilling to face the knife, when it is circumcision time, is caught and initiated forcefully. Boys are under great pressure to submit to it. Men who are suspected of being uncircumcised are stripped naked and given the rite then and there. Thus some educated Bagisu will have the operation done in a hospital.

Circumcision is honored among the Bagisu. They are proud to undergo this test of bravery into manhood. No other Bantu tribe in Uganda performs this rite. Among the Nilo-Hamitic, only the Sebei still practice circumcision. In fact no marriage is valid with them unless the man has been circumcised. Both of these tribes do not dream of giving up this custom.

Bagisu girls, unlike neighboring Sebei, are not circumcised. Their proof of bravery is to pass through a painful process of scarification by cutting keloids on the abdomen and head. The skin is pinched into a fold and a needle is drawn through it. Then the hole is filled with ashes. When the wounds are healed, the keloids stand out as hard peas. These scarification marks are cut in lines running down the abdomen and on the forehead running down the temples. They are commonly seen on older women and less among the younger. A sign that more are leaving this practice behind.

This pearl of Africa is tarnished further still by the worship of ancestor spirits. It is very evident among the Nilotic tribes to the north. Shrines are erected to honor and appease the spirits. At their "ngoma" (dances) songs are sung to exalt their feats. Ancestral spirits are very much a part of everyday life. They can bring about evil or good in their daily walk. When misfortune strikes, the witchdoctor is consulted to determine which spirit it is and what is needed to correct the situation. Satan has many bound to the past, to rituals for the spirits of the dead. But Christ has set others free and given them a life with an upward look.

In the past numerous tribes throughout Africa practiced cannibalism. The Teso, Bagisu, Lango and others in Uganda were part of that number. During the days of British administration this practice was forbidden. The result was that those who still craved human flesh turned to alternate ways. Instead of capturing their foe and then cooking him in a pot, they carved up their dead for a meal. This led to the digging up of fresh graves to remove the corpse when no immediate dead were available.

While in Bukedi I often wondered why there are cement slabs scattered here and there in open fields. Finally I learned that they are graves! Just like the ones I have seen on George's yard and others. At one time houses had stood there. Today only the graves remain. To prevent their dead being robbed from the grave a cement slab is placed over it. What about those who cannot afford the price of cement? They take turns watching over the grave of the recently deceased for the first three or four nights to discourage any cannibal in the neighbourhood.

Drunkenness, polygamy, circumcision, ancestral worship, witchcraft, cannibalism and demon possession are deep rooted. They are real obstacles in the lives of those seeking to follow Christ. Satan is not willing to release a single soul from his kingdom of darkness. These practices still tarnish the pearl today. My prayer is that the Ugandans will allow Christ to bring a lustre to this part of Africa. In order to achieve this Satan must be bound. In the power of Christ's name it can be done. There is no other way!

I personally was challenged by Satan soon after our arrival to Uganda. It is midnight and I am awakened from a dream I am having in which I was attempting to bind the power of Satan. He had appeared in the corner of our living room. I was afraid but determined at the same time to defeat him. He avoided me and kept slipping away each time. Then I awoke. The same feeling persists!

I get out of bed and walk over to where I saw Satan in my dream. His presence is very real! I also feel the fear I had in the dream. I commence to bind him in the name of Jesus. I am not going to let him overpower me! Then he endeavours to slip away but I persist. Finally I succeed! I have finished what I failed to do in my dream. Satan leaves the house defeated. I now sense the presence of the Lord, it fills the room! Hallelujah!

This transpired soon after moving into our home on Muyenga. I learned from this encounter with Satan that in the name of Jesus I can bind his evil forces in Uganda. Whenever we met on subsequent occasions I knew I could render him powerless each time if I persisted. The result was that many demon-possessed have been released from bondage. But the road is still long and rugged before this country can become the lustrious pearl God desires it to be.

Jesus said to them, "Go into all the world and preach the good news to all creation. Whoever believes and is baptized will be saved, but whoever does not believe will be condemned. And these signs will accompany those who believe: In my name they will drive out demons, they will speak in new tongues, they will pick up snakes with their hands and when they drink deadly poison it will not hurt them at all. They will place their hands on sick people and they will get well." (Mark 16:15-18)

# Chapter Twenty
# Running To Keep Up!

Tim and Colleen are in the front seat while Tiffany is sitting between grandma and grandpa in the back. We are on our way to the border. Time has come for Marion and I to take our furlough. What a change that will be! Rather shocking to say the least. The comparison between such things as roads, sanitation, punctuality and security, to mention a few, will be astonishing. Just the same I will miss Uganda for it is here that God made the book of Acts come alive before my very eyes!

The promise which Marion and I received four years ago, as we stepped off the plane at Entebbe, has been fulfilled. He was with us each step of the way! And most of those steps were spent, not in walking, but in running. Running to keep up with the Holy Spirit who was ever moving, opening doors into different tribes and districts for me to deliver the gospel. Thank you Lord for the strength you constantly gave me to keep running. Without this it would not have been possible.

It did not take long and the work began to expand.

The number of the churches grew from two to where it is today at two hundred and sixty-two, from seventy believers to over 13,035! The pressure of this rapid growth and the concern for all these churches would have been too much for me had it not been for you Lord. And my prayer is that you will continue to add to your church here in Uganda in spite of the countless hardships that still exist. I do not read in Acts though where such things interfered with its growth. Instead, they contributed to its expansion!

I am so grateful for the leaders who have sprung up from the midst of this young church. Without their dedication and willingness the Holy Spirit would not have opened as many doors as He did. But when the Lord asked, "Who will go?" there was someone who was ready to answer, "Here am I, send me." To begin with though it was just Marion and Rufus who accompanied me to this mountainous task of making the Church of God known in Uganda.

A year later Ephraim Tumusiime joined us on our safaris, while his companion Elijah Rwanika accepted the call to pastor the church at Kasubi in Kampala. With his gift of teaching Ephraim assisted us tremendously in our T.E.E. (Theological Education by Extension) program which is in full swing even now. It is a course of books specially prepared for training pastors and lay leaders who are unable to attend an institution. Instead of going off to Bible School, it comes to them in their home. This program has given back-bone to our church. We appreciate this well planned course.

God recognized that the run was becoming too long for our national evangelist, Rufus, and brings in a relay team. Francis Makosia answers the call, picks up the baton and runs with the gospel in eastern Uganda from the islands in Lake Victoria through Samia, Busoga, Budama, over the mountainous ranges in Bugisu, Sebei and onto the plains of Karamoja. Ah, what stamina! Wilson Owiny takes it from there in northern Uganda through the bushlands of Teso, Lango, Acholi and across the Nile River into Alur. Finally Godfrey Muhwezi accepts the challenge and carries it in western Uganda meandering among the hills of Kigezi, Akole and on to Toro in the shadow of the Ruwenzori Mountains.

This means now that Rufus can concentrate in central Uganda. Since the war we have been making in-roads into this once troubled district of Buganda. And there is Bunyoro where Paulo Mwendwa keeps going on. He is our longest serving pastor for the Church of God in Uganda. Without his call for help, the Lord may never have laid the burden of Uganda upon my heart. In Bukedi, George Muzei works feverishly and has the largest number of churches in a district with the highest total of Christians. Then there are other leaders pressing on towards the goal to win the prize for which God has called them heaven-ward in Christ Jesus. Praise the Lord for all of them.

All I have been able to accomplish, of course, could not have been possible without the assistance of my wife. She persevered with my determination to reach the four corners of Uganda for Christ. Accompanying me on almost every journey I made up country, she has tasted the same food I ate and washed in the same water that was brought for bathing which was taken in an enclosure erected from grass or "bati" (tin). She did not even complain about latrines which came in all shapes and sizes, some so narrow you could not turn around, others too low to stand erect. I could not help but wonder— how far have the termites gotten with the timbers below my feet?

Marion has slept in the same narrow, rickety bed which had a hen with her chicks near our heads. The rooster was early and awakened us at three-thirty in the morning! Bats and rats were always a nuisance, shortening still the hours of the night. There were times we awakened with dust on our faces from the grass roof being eaten by termites.

Whenever possible the Nissan patrol was our bedroom. Crawling in and out daily for a week or more on each safari was not one of her favorite exercises, I am sure. She had to learn how to undress and dress in a sitting position. I found too that it was quite a feat to wriggle into trousers while lying on my back! There were always on-lookers. We gradually got used to them.

Marion has helped to keep the districts informed of what God is doing throughout the country by publishing the "Sower" which is handed out to the pastors and lay men to read and pass around in their churches. She has always been interested in the work, whether with me on the road or remaining at home. So much so that upon returning home fatigued, ready for a night's sleep on a soft bed, she keeps me awake for hours persistent in knowing what transpired at each seminar. Finally satisfied, she drops into a peaceful sleep. And what about me? Sleep has wandered off and I cannot locate it! I am wide awake, re-living what I have just come from up country.

My wife is a great hostess, in spite of the power and water failures we experience in Kampala. The door is open to guests with something to drink and eat provided in short order. How often I have returned from a safari, which I made alone, bringing back Rufus and/or someone else without her knowledge. This she took in stride, and a bed was soon made ready for the night. It was extra work for her but she always rose to the occasion. In fact, the first year and a half, four seminars were held on our premises! They slept everywhere. When our house had no more space for them, tents were erected. Eventually as the number of churches increased in the districts, the seminars were then held there. I am sure she often felt as I have felt—where will my next ounce of strength come from? But He was there, the One who promised to be with us each step of the way.

There were very few places to take her alone in Uganda. The parks are miles away and yet too dangerous for sight-seeing because of rebels ambushing vehicles and robbing their occupants. The nights in Kampala are unsafe, so we spent them at home behind doors habitually locked at seven each evening. Gunfire and ululating of unfortunate victims being looted then serenaded us through the night. Not to hear gun shots at night is an exception.

The only compensation I have to offer her for the lonely hours spent in Kampala was to have her attend the International Women's Convention a year ago in America where she had an opportunity to soak up some spiritual blessings. Plus a visit with Mark and her mother for a few days before returning. Then, having her mother finally step upon African soil and be with us for a month this year, was a dream come true for all of us. Especially for Colleen and Tiffany, for it brought together four generations right here in Uganda! A rare occasion indeed. A safari to Tanzania was made so that Mom could see where we and the Baums, who accompanied her, had labored for years. The prayers of Lydia Schwartz have touched His throne daily on our behalf.

God has protected us so wonderfully from the enemies.

The safaris I made that separated us for days, He not only gave me safety on the road but her protection as well at home. For this I am so thankful to you Lord. You are so faithful in your promises!

With the work mushrooming as it did, I discovered I would not have time for the manual side of it. Travelling to seminars, teaching classes and holding services, plus my office work, was demanding most of my time. I found this out when the church at Kinyonga was being built in memory of Marion's father, that I would not be able to cope with the added responsibility of constructing buildings which loomed on the horizon. There was the pressing need to erect the Day Care Center at Kasubi. What to do?

I took this burden to you Lord and early one morning you revealed the couple to me. The man was a licensed contractor in building and she a graduate at Anderson College with a degree in early childhood. The perfect couple for the task before us. And what made it even more super was that they were M.K.'s (missionary kids). This should help in their orientation. If they agreed when I call them, I knew it truly was God's will.

When I phoned Tim and asked him, the reply was "Sure, when should I come!" That was it. It was not long after that they arrived and have been here ever since. Tim and Colleen Stevenson met at Rift Valley Academy in Kenya, back in the seventies. His parents were missionaries at Mombasa, Kenya, during this time. Little did Tim and Colleen know that the love they had for each other then would prove to be lasting, and that one day it would lead them back to where it started—in Africa!

It is rare, and because it is rare, I treasure it all the more—to have my daugher and her daughter with me in the mission field! When we left for Uganda, my heart nearly broke when it came time to say goodbye to the kids. They had always been a part of our Africa. Two years later when they informed us of the date they will be arriving for a visit, Marion and I were like two little children waiting for their gifts to be opened the night before Christmas. What a treat! We saved and scrimped to make our holiday together a memorable one. And it was. Visiting our old stamping grounds in Tanzania was one of the high-lights!

Well, when Kirk and Karen stayed on and began working with World Vision International in Sudan, we were excited about it as they. Kirk who was born in Tanzania, loves Africa as much as I do. And now he is back in the land he has learned to love. We will be able to get together now and then. Kirk and Karen Hoffman met at Rift Valley Academy as well, and it all began there too. Her parents were missionaries in Burundi during those years.

Then when Tim and Colleen came and moved in with us, that was the icing on the cake! For two years the Lord has granted what fathers just dream about, namely, to have again his daughter about the place. I had her for eighteen eyars while a missionary to Tanzania and Kenya. She was exactly a year old when she came to Africa. And now she has presented me with a grand-daughter. I knew it would be a girl! Thanks Colleen. She reminds me so much of you.

Tiffany's birth was heralded by the sound of gun fire from outside Nsambya hospital at nine forty-five in the evening, on June 25, 1986. Marion and I anxiously await-ed her arrival in the waiting room, while Tim was with Colleen in the delivery room. We did not have long to wait for soon she was in our arms. Our first grandchild! I should have felt old right then. A grandfather! But no, instead, I returned to yester-years and was cradling Colleen in my arms again.

It is sweet what Tiffany has done for me since her arrival. Not to spoil her, I try to keep my distance as much as I am able. But I will get blamed for it anyway so why try too hard. My many safaris up country have denied me much of her time. At first she would forget me and make shy when I returned. And then, to my joy, she eventually kept remembering me.

But to be away for a year is too much to expect. I shall miss her so very much. Will she miss me? I shall miss her blue eyes staring back at me over the breakfast table. I shall miss carrying her outside to see our two German Shepherds. I wanted them to get used to her and she them. The relationship is good thus far. They should be "kali" (mean) but actually they are mostly bark and no bite. While with Simba and Chui (Lion and Leopard), I would mention their names to her and add, "Bow-wow." It was not long that when I picked her up she would say, "Bow-wow," letting me know she wanted to go out and see them.

I shall miss her coming into my office and tugging at my pant leg wanting up. She reaches for the typewriter or scatters the pens here and there. Marion remarked one day, "You never allowed your children to do that." I like to believe I did. Maybe that is why I allow my grandchild to do it now. Trying to make amends. It takes years to mellow one sometimes. That is why grandpa loves Tiffany so much!

May this book I am dedicating to her be a reminder someday of my love for her and the good times she gave me during her first year and my fourth together in perilous Uganda.

Well, here we are at the border. Beyond the big gate

lies Kenya then Canada and Mark, whom I have not seen since his visit two years ago. We have passed through here many times in the past four years, mainly for groceries as the selection in Kampala has been poor, and what there was cost three times as much! Today, it is not for a day or a week, but for a year. Farewell Uganda! Be not so harsh on my granddaughter, daughter and son-in-law. Try to be more gentle with them.

And, Lord, do not tire of answering my prayers. Please look after them. They will now be alone, and they may have to run as well to keep up. As you saw us through some perilous times, do so for them. The situation has not changed much in struggling Uganda, Lord. Set your guardian angels about them for surely they too will find themselves amid perils often.